MINDFUL
& STRESS
LESS

50 ways to deal with your (crazy) life

Gina M. Biegel, MA, LMFT

SHAMBHALA
Boulder 2018

Shambhala Publications, Inc.
4720 Walnut Street
Boulder, Colorado 80301
www.shambhala.com

9 8 7 6 5 4 3 2 1

First Edition
Printed in the United States of America

♾ This edition is printed on acid-free paper that meets the American
National Standards Institute Z39.48 Standard.
♻ Shambhala makes every effort to print on recycled paper. For
more information please visit www.shambhala.com.
Distributed in the United States by Penguin Random House LLC and in
Canada by Random House of Canada Ltd

Designed by Liz Quan

LIBRARY OF CONGRESS CATALOGING-IN-PUBLICATION DATA
Names: Biegel, Gina M., author.
Title: Be mindful and stress less: 50 ways to deal with your (crazy) life /
  Gina M. Biegel, MA, LMFT.
Description: First edition. | Boulder: Shambhala, [2018]
Identifiers: LCCN 2017021381 | ISBN 9781611804942 (pbk.: alk. paper)
Subjects: LCSH: Stress management for teenagers—Juvenile literature. |
Self-consciousness (Awareness)—Juvenile literature. | Resilience
  (Personality trait)—Juvenile literature. | Mindfulness
  (Psychology)—Juvenile literature.
Classification: LCC BF724.3.S86 B538 2018 | DDC 155.5/191—dc23
LC record available at https://lccn.loc.gov/2017021381

For Tomas O'Sullivan:
Although I never had the privilege of meeting you, you have made a profound and lasting impact on my life. You left too soon. You give me purpose and a renewed intention to my work.

If I can help even one teen learn that mindfulness-based practices provide another way out of pain and suffering, I will have honored my life's purpose.

CONTENTS

PART TWO
Self-CARE: Self-Compassion, Self-Acceptance, Self-Respect, Self-Esteem   52

PART THREE
ACORN: Always Consider Other Responses Now

INTRODUCTION

What Does It Mean to Be Mindful?

William James, the first educator to offer a psychology course in the United States, said, "This life is worth living, we can say, since it is what we make it."

I wrote this book as a professional because I am a therapist, a researcher, and a writer on mindfulness and related well-being topics that help teens and young adults manage their stress. But it's also a very personal book because I have put my heart and soul into it. I include many tidbits of information I now know that could have helped me when I was younger.

I wrote this book specifically for teens and young adults—for you—because life can be amazing. It can also be downright awful, deplorable, unbearable, frightening, and miserable. This is a guidebook and a compass to help you navigate every moment of your life. What you'll learn here are life skills and lessons that you can bring to every age, stage, and situation for the rest of your life. The truth is these are topics that most people still grapple with.

I believe that teens and young adults are like sponges and have the ability to understand and take in the concepts and offerings throughout this book. I know this because I have seen it happen to thousands of teens and young adults I have worked with over the last fifteen years.

Your life is going on every second of every day. Whether you want to be part of it or not is up to you. These formative years can be a very difficult time; figuring out who you are and who you want to be, not to mention managing everyone else's expectations, can be overwhelming and even painful at times. The skills in this book can give you a road map for how to navigate your life mindfully.

Mindfulness is noticing your thoughts, feelings, and physical sensations in the present moment without harmful judgment. Instead of the natural tendency to be on automatic pilot, it is about waking up to your life, as it is unfolding, moment to moment. Mindfulness does not imply that you will be slow, quiet, or perfectly still in every moment—otherwise there would be zombie- or sloth-like people walking around. It is about present-moment awareness. When you are more mindful, you can be present to many more moments of your life. Life moments, even if painful, can provide opportunities for you to grow, learn, change, and thrive.

I encourage you to read this book from beginning to end. Mark, highlight, bookmark, or take pictures of anything that seems most relevant so you can return to it as needed. This book is separated into three sections, and each builds on the preceding one.

The first section, "PAWS," is about paying attention to life with your senses. When you pay attention to any or all of your senses in any given moment, you are being mindful. The foundational skills in this section help you to live in the now and to bring mindfulness to the relationships you have with yourself, others, and the world around you.

The second section, "Self-CARE," is about having compassion, acceptance, respect, and esteem for yourself, which is necessary before you can truly be there for others in these ways. Self-CARE teaches you to be there for yourself; to learn what resources, wants, and needs you have; and to use your strengths, resources, and the skills in this section to meet your wants and needs as they arise. Being in a relationship with yourself in these ways can help you to manage the difficulties that life may throw at you. The Self-CARE section will also better enable you to be present in your relationships with others, model for others how to care for themselves, and allow you to be more compassionate, accepting, and respecting of other people.

The third section, "ACORN," is about the value of always considering other responses now before you act toward yourself or others. When you use the ACORN acronym, you have the power and control to decide how you want to respond to people, places, things, or situations in your life; instead of the tendency to automatically react. ACORN helps you learn about and navigate the landscape of your mind—including both your thoughts and feelings. You can more easily get unstuck and rightsized about the painful, upsetting, worrisome, and stressful moments of your life.

MINDFUL   TAKEAWAY

Every moment is a new opportunity to pay attention, to reason, to decide, to respond, and to live.

PART ONE

PAWS

Pay Attention With Senses

PAWS is a way to be mindful of everything in your life. If you are paying attention to any of your five senses, you are in the present—right here, right now— which means being mindful.

Jon Kabat-Zinn, the creator of the Mindfulness-Based Stress Reduction program for adults, titled one of his books *Coming to Our Senses: Healing Ourselves and the World Through Mindfulness*. The easiest way to be mindful is to pay attention to your senses in everything you do. If you are paying attention to any of your five senses (sight, sound, smell, touch, and taste), you are being mindful. People perceive and make sense of their world through their senses.

Mindfulness is about waking up to and living your life as if it really mattered—which it does. You can be mindful from the minute you wake up until the minute you go to sleep. This section helps you tune in to what is already around you that you may not even be noticing.

PAWS is about building the foundations of mindfulness. The foundational skills in this section provide the necessary teachings for you to benefit from the sections that follow. Once you have this foundation, you can begin to understand how mindfulness can be an integral part of how you live your life; of the relationships you have; and of how you make sense of the people, places, things, and situations as they present themselves.

As you go through the chapters in this section, you can start to experience mindfulness in action and what it is to be mindful.

1

PAWS: SIGHT

Before you read any further, look around you. What do you see right now?

What is on your body—clothes, shoes, jewelry, anything else? Notice not only what is in front of you but also what is behind you and to your sides. What is farther away? What is up close? Close your eyes. What can you see through your closed eyelids? What do you see now that you didn't see before you read this?

The next time you are in a dark room, notice what it is like to see virtually nothing. Over time, your eyes will begin to focus, and you will begin to see shapes and forms.

Most of us take the sense of sight for granted because it is something we do automatically. Consider, if you didn't have the sense of sight, what it would be like for you? To expand on your awareness of sight, read on.

zooming and focus

You can choose your focus, viewing the world as if you are looking through a camera lens. You can zoom out to look at the whole picture or landscape, taking in everything. You can also zoom in to focus closely on one thing, like one piece of a larger puzzle.

Right now, look around you. What do you see when you zoom out and see as much as you possibly can? Now, pick one thing to focus on and zoom in, noticing everything you can about that one thing. What do things look like when you zoom out? What do things look like when you zoom in?

You can compare zooming out and in to the way you perceive and manage situations in life. For example, when you are faced with a difficult situation—a conflict with another person—are you able to zoom out and in? Can you look at all the sides and points of view for a given situation by zooming out, seeing all perspectives? Can you zoom in to see each person's experience, side, or position? The ability to zoom both out and in, and knowing when you aren't able to do either or both, can greatly impact your ability to problem solve and manage difficult situations.

When you look through a camera lens, things are often blurry or out of focus at first. To get them in focus, you need to adjust the camera lens until you can see things clearly.

Similarly, in life it can take time to adjust your focus to see a situation clearly. At times, you just can't seem to focus clearly on a situation no matter how hard you try. When have you found it hard to see situations in focus? The next time it is hard for you to see things clearly or focus, consider taking a step away from the situation or a brief pause, and then try refocusing. Sometimes a change in perspective or a moment away from the intensity of a situation can make all the difference in seeing something more clearly and as it is.

how do you see things?

What are the details—forms, shapes, textures, and/or colors—of what you see? Once you see something, how do you make sense of it to know that a cup is a cup or this spherical thing is a spoon? The process of making sense of something is conceptualization. How you conceptualize is based on your past experiences, memories, knowledge, and your current mood.

Take clouds, for example. You can look up at the sky and see that the shapes moving across it are what you know to be clouds. If you are in a miserable mood because you got into a disagreement with a good friend, you may pay attention only to one patch of clouds. What you might not notice is that the rest of the sky is sunny, and the patch of clouds has already passed over you and is moving on.

MINDFUL TAKEAWAY

Work on zooming out and in of situations to see things from different points of view. To put things in focus, consider taking a step away or a brief pause, and then refocus. Use these tools to see people, places, things, and situations more clearly.

2

PAWS: HEARING

What can you hear right now? What noises are in your surroundings? Now close your eyes and listen. Did you hear anything more?

sound practice

Sounds can shift and change the longer you listen to them. They can widen, deepen, and unfold. You will probably hear the loudest and closest sounds first, followed by the softer and more distant ones. As you continue to listen, sounds become clearer. Many sounds often get missed. For example, the air conditioner, heater, fan, and computer emit *ambient noises*—sounds that are there but unnoticed have become background noise. For thirty to sixty seconds, listen for all the sounds you can. Consider what sounds might now be present that you didn't even think about or hear at first.

What did you hear early on in the sound practice?

What did you hear a little later? Did you notice any ambient noises? If so, what were they?

information that sounds provide

It is normal not to notice every single sound all the time. You could be busy or doing something that doesn't require you to be aware of all the sounds around you. But it is important to pay attention to sounds that have some use or provide you with information.

SOUNDS CAN SERVE A PURPOSE	
Sounds Can	Example
Alert you when something isn't safe	Fire alarm
Calm you or provide you with a sense of peace	Water running down a stream
Distract you	Music
Bring you joy and happiness	Friends laughing and joking around

What sounds alert you? What sounds calm you? What sounds distract you? What sounds bring you joy and happiness?

Depending on the situation, a sound can serve more than one purpose. Music can alert you if you use it as an alarm in the morning. It can calm you if you tune in to a channel that plays chill music. It is a distraction when you turn it up loud to forget the fight you just had with someone. It can bring you happiness, peace, and joy when you sing along with it in the car.

technology awareness

Mobile phones are such a commonplace part of people's lives and have so many uses that their sounds often gets overlooked or unnoticed. Even when a phone is on silent mode, it can still provide a vibrating tone. It isn't that you need to keep your phone off all the time, but it can be beneficial to notice how it can impact you. At night, phones can keep you up or wake you. It can be difficult to have a pause from technology if your phone is always on. Phone alerts can be another type of ambient noise.

MINDFUL   TAKEAWAY

As you walk through your day today, notice the sounds that might otherwise go unnoticed. To be silent requires the complete absence of all sound. Consider if and when you are ever actually in silence.

3
PAWS: SMELL

Sniff the air. Do you smell anything? If you sniff the air and smell nothing, then that is what nothing smells like. Notice that when you sniff, you are moving air in and out of your nose, which means you are breathing.

pleasant, unpleasant, and neutral smells

Smell is an interesting sense because people usually associate smells with like or dislike. You can categorize smells as pleasant, unpleasant, and neutral. A smell that is pleasant may reference something enjoyable, like cookies in the oven or a fragrant candle. A smell that is unpleasant may reference something disliked, like sweaty clothes in a locker room. Neutral smells are those that don't trigger an association of pleasant or unpleasant. They are often unnoticed. For example, the times you sniff the air and don't smell anything could be considered neutral.

Scents are tied to your individual memories and differ from person to person. Think of your top five pleasant and unpleasant smells. What makes those scents pleasant or unpleasant to you?

smells and expectations

When you walk into a kitchen, what do you expect to smell? When you walk into a locker room, what do you expect to smell? Because scents are tied to your memories, you will often predict or assume what a specific area will smell like based on your past experiences. You can expect that when you walk onto a grassy field, you will smell grass. However, if it is Astroturf, your expectation may be thrown off because the field will not have the smell you know of as grass.

—MINDFUL   TAKEAWAY—

Remember, you can sniff the air anytime and notice what you smell. You can deepen your experience by considering whether the smell is something pleasant, unpleasant, or neutral to you. When you're thrown off by unexpected smells, take note of them.

4
PAWS: TOUCH

What can you feel right now with your fingers and hands? Your clothes? This book? What is your body touching? Your chair, if you are sitting? The ground, if you are standing?

Wherever you are right now, what is the temperature? Is it cold, hot, or warm? Would you describe it some other way? You can tell what the temperature is because you can feel it; your sense of touch is engaged.

Experiment and touch whatever you want in your immediate surroundings. What is the texture of what you are touching? Would you describe it as smooth, rough, hard, soft, or something else?

objects and people
There are quite a few ways to notice the sense of touch. You can touch objects with your fingers and hands, toes and feet, and even your entire body. Conversely, an object can touch you—for example, if you stub your toe

because you weren't aware of the raised and uneven pavement in front of you. You can also interact with others through touch. A high five, a hug, and a handshake are all examples of touch with other people. Think about a typical day. What objects or people are you normally in contact with?

touch and safety

Notice how your body responds to an initial touch, whether it is from an object or a person. When you first experience a touch, your body immediately assesses whether it is safe or unsafe. Given this automatic response, you decide what to do next. If you sit on a chair that is unstable and wobbly, you will most likely notice it is unsafe and then adjust and sit in a spot that is safe and comfortable. Similarly, if someone you care about gives you a hug, you will probably hug back because it feels safe. Conversely, if someone you don't know leans in to give you a hug, you may back off because it feels unsafe.

touch and mood

Touch can evoke different feeling states: enjoyment, happiness, anger, and frustration, to name a few. Think of the objects you enjoy touching. Think of the objects you dislike touching.

Touch from other people can also evoke different feeling states: love, like, dislike, and hate, for example. Think of people you enjoy connecting with. Think of others you would prefer to have no connection with. You probably tend to hold on or cling to what you enjoy, and resist or push away what you don't like.

grounding by touch

When you aren't in a good space (for example, when you are sad, angry, anxious, depressed, worried, or frustrated), you may be in your head too much. At times like these, it can be hard to be present in the moment. Grounding focal points—such as your fingers, hands, and feet—are grounding points you can focus on to get out of your head. These grounding points are always with you. Focusing on any of them can often ground you to the present moment.

Notice the air that is around your fingers and hands. Notice the sensations and energy that are present here. When you stand, you are touching the ground. When you walk, you are touching the ground. Hence the reason why, when walking, your feet are a strong grounding focal point: because you are touching the ground. Walking can be useful when you need emotional grounding. You can emotionally ground yourself by taking a walk. If you have the opportunity and it is safe to do so, walking on the grass barefoot is particularly helpful to ground you when experiencing difficult emotional states.

grabbing an ice cube

Sometimes people turn to self-harming behaviors when they are in bad spaces emotionally. Self-harming behaviors don't fix any problems. What's more, these behaviors usually make things worse!

You can always grab an ice cube if you're feeling a need to engage in a harming behavior. Hold the ice cube in one hand until it melts. Doing this can often provide a result similar to that of many harming behaviors: there is a numbing—a feeling of physical rather than emotional pain—but it isn't dangerous or harmful in any way. *Go grab an ice cube instead of self-harming!*

MINDFUL TAKEAWAY

It is helpful to pay attention to your grounding focal points (fingers, hands, and feet) when you are feeling upset or are stuck in your own head, ruminating about a person, place, thing, or situation.

5

PAWS: TASTE

What do you taste in your mouth right now? If you think you are not tasting anything, that is what nothing tastes like.

taste sensations

There are five main types of taste sensations: sour, sweet, salty, bitter, and savory (otherwise referred to as umami). Your mouth, tongue, and taste buds allow you to recognize specific taste sensations. When you put food or drink in your mouth, your body automatically begins to produce saliva as it prepares to digest.

Think of two foods you have tasted that fall into each of the five categories: (1) sour, (2) sweet, (3) salty, (4) bitter, and (5) savory.

Which of these taste categories do you like most? Which of these categories do you dislike the most?

liking and disliking tastes

Your current and previous experiences of liking or disliking a taste will lead you to cling to the taste or have an aversion to it. If you like a taste, such as chocolate, you will often want more of it or even cling to its taste once you have it. On the other hand, when you taste something you dislike, you will generally try to end that taste quickly.

The term *impermanence* describes how things change, how they aren't permanent or enduring. For example, the sweet taste from a ripe strawberry is impermanent. It will be strong at first and then begin to fade. It is interesting to notice how you feel when tastes fade, shift, and change.

If you have tasted something before, you probably have expectations of what it should taste like. Try an experiment: when you taste a food you have had many times, try to notice the taste of it *this time,* instead of thinking what it should be like or what it is going to be like.

MINDFUL TAKEAWAY

The next time you put something in your mouth, bring full attention to the taste you notice. Recognize your desires to cling to, or push away, certain tastes.

6

TAKING MINDFUL BITES

Here are some questions to ask yourself about the way you eat:

- Do you find that you often don't taste your food?

- Are you rushing when you eat?

- Do you often eat while you are doing something else?

- Do you notice if you are full or even still hungry?

- Do you go to get more of your meal and realize you've finished it already and hadn't noticed?

mindless eating

If you answered yes to any of these questions, it is likely that you are eating mindlessly or on autopilot, eating without paying attention to what you're doing. It is common to eat this way. If you aren't paying attention to what you're doing while you're doing it, you aren't in the present.

one-bite practice, part I

Eat one bite of food the way you normally do. Please don't continue reading until you have eaten that bite.

Now consider the following questions:

- Were you doing anything else at the same time?

- What did the food taste like?

- Is the food something you like or dislike?

- Is this something you eat frequently?

- Were you hungry or full when you ate the bite?

- Can you remember what you noticed with each of your senses (sight, sound, smell, touch, and taste) as you ate that bite?

- Did you find that you were aware of, and present to, that bite or mostly unaware?

mindful eating

Mindful eating involves noticing what and how you eat. It doesn't mean you must eat everything slowly. What it means is that you pay attention to what you're eating while you're eating it.

A component of mindful eating is to notice whether you are full or still hungry. Paying attention to each of the different senses (sight, sound, smell, touch, and taste) while eating can help. A good way to start eating mindfully is to work on one bite of every meal.

one-bite practice, part II

Now mindfully eat one bite of the same food you just tasted. Please don't continue reading until you have mindfully eaten that bite.

Consider the following questions:

- What are the differences between the two bites?

- Look back at the questions in part I. Are your answers any different now?

People often see a variety of results when they eat mindfully:

- They are more aware of when they are full or when they are eating when not actually hungry.

- They can notice if they are eating for comfort.

- They notice if they like or dislike what they are eating.

- They can tell if they are eating automatically or are more present to what they are eating.

- They can notice each of their senses, if they choose to, while they eat.

Just some food for thought!

MINDFUL TAKEAWAY

Pay attention to different bites of food at each meal this week. When you eat mindfully, do you notice that you dislike foods you thought you liked? Or even better, that you like foods you thought you disliked?

7
SWEET TREAT

When you eat something sweet today, do it mindfully. Try to savor it. Notice what thoughts arise when you taste it. Notice how it feels to try to eat it mindfully. What is that experience like?

savor the sweetness
There are many opportunities to savor the sweetness of what you eat. You can extend this savoring of sweet things to savoring enjoyable, pleasant, and just plain good life moments. Many positive moments in life may be noticed and dismissed or may pass by without being truly savored and taken in. Why not take in the sweetness of good moments?

planting seeds, growing flowers
When you sow a flower seed and care for it, you are enabling the seed to sprout, grow, and flower. Similarly, with life experiences you can have a positive expe-

rience, take it in, and truly savor the sweetness of that experience. You can take in positive experiences and turn them into lasting beneficial resources by noticing, attending, and holding on to that experience.

growing resources: your flower bouquet

When you collect flowers, eventually you can make an entire flower bouquet. If you grow your resources by taking in beneficial experiences, over time they collect and create a "bouquet" of resources you can turn to. You then have a reserve that can assist you in managing and getting through difficult times.

noticing flowers in the weeds

You may have read the children's book *Alexander and the Terrible, Horrible, No Good, Very Bad Day* by Judith Viorst. Even when you are having a day like Alexander's, you can choose to notice and take in the good, the pleasant, and the positive.

It can be hard to see flowers among the weeds. Translating this to everyday life, sometimes it can be hard to savor sweet moments if a lot of crappy stuff is going on. Your focus might only be on the weeds or what isn't working, instead of the few flowers hidden among the weeds and on what *is* working.

weeds have a purpose

What if a weed was a flower in disguise? Sometimes weeds are beautiful; they might look like flowers even if they are technically weeds. You might not notice what purpose a weed can provide you, or what flower or positive experience you can take from a difficult situation.

Sometimes there are weeds that have thorns, are prickly, or give the appearance that you might want to stay away from them because they are harmful. In life, some things that might appear dangerous or scary are so, and they should be noticed for what they are—weeds.

your basic needs

There is often more right with you than there is wrong. Consider the following basic needs that are currently being met:

- Did you wake up today?

- Do you have a roof over your head?

- Do you have food when you're hungry?

- Do you have water to drink when you're thirsty?

- Do you have clean air to breathe?

- Do you have electricity?

It can be hard to notice all that is going right when one thing is going wrong. Try to notice the people or situations that are positive or supportive in your life right now. Here are some areas to think about:

- Relationships—family, peer, or romantic

- Health

- Freedom

- Education

- Career

- Financial—support, security, or stability

- Sense of community

- Sense of connection

MINDFUL   TAKEAWAY

Every day is full of opportunities to have or create positive experiences that turn into lasting beneficial resources. Savor the sweetness of things and take in the good!

8

PAY ATTENTION TO COLOR

Try to be a rainbow in someone's cloud.

—Maya Angelou

Are you someone who pays attention to the rainbow or someone who pays attention to the cloud? It is interesting to consider how colors impact you. Additionally, if you tend to focus on the cloud, learn to use the skills in this book to start looking at, or for, the rainbows.

color awareness

Colors can greatly impact how someone feels. Bright colors, like red or orange, can offer a felt sense of energy whereas blue or green might provide a sense of being more relaxed or calm. Colors can provide or instill a certain feeling or even affect the direction of thoughts and behaviors.

Different colors can evoke different moods or feelings. Colors can be very powerful in affecting your emotions and thoughts and, in turn, your actions. Look around you right now. Notice which colors stand out to you. Do any of these colors evoke a specific emotion for you?

When you read the following words, what colors come to your mind?

- Sadness, hurt

- Frustration, anger

- Anxiety, worry

- Exclusion, discomfort, isolation

- Love, happiness, peace

- Contentment, comfort, ease

- Silliness, humor

warm and cool colors

Reds, oranges, and yellows—colors at the warm end of the color spectrum—are often connected to the sun, heat, and fire. Colors at the other end of the spectrum, like greens and blues, are cooler, and they are often connected to the water, sky, and ice. What thoughts come up for you when you think of warm and cool colors? Do you think of a certain time of year? The weather? Do you associate different colors with certain moods? If so, which color for which mood? Nature? Types of clothing? Various sports? Something else?

What is your favorite color? Look at your surroundings right now. See if you can find that color. Is it on your clothes? Is it behind you? Is it in front of you? For the rest of the day, try to notice when you see this color.

Can you recall some of your favorite memories that are associated with this color? What are those memories?

MINDFUL TAKEAWAY

Open your awareness to the different colors that are present in new and novel places, as well as those places where you are all the time. Notice how different colors improve or worsen your mood.

9

SENSE THE DAY

Observe, record, tabulate, communicate. Use your five senses. Learn to see, learn to hear, learn to feel, learn to smell, and know that by practice alone you can become expert.

—Sir William Osler, physician

You are mindful when you are aware of any of your senses. When you take in your surroundings through paying attention to your senses, you are more spaciously aware.

spacious and directed awareness

Spacious awareness is an awareness of what is literally in your space. It is when you become more spaciously aware of, for example, your surroundings—what is in front of or behind you. Additionally, you can become more aware of your surroundings through utilizing your senses—sight, smell, touch, taste, and hearing.

Spacious awareness is a profoundly valuable aspect of mindfulness, and it requires using your senses to be receptive to and accepting of whatever comes into your environment.

Once you become aware of your space and surroundings, you must then decide where you want to focus and direct your attention. *Directed awareness* is another aspect of mindfulness, where you deliberately pay attention to something in your environment. You can focus on the big picture, on the entire landscape, or on just one piece of the picture. This is where spacious awareness shifts into a more directed awareness. You take in what you see and decide where you want to put your attention and focus. If you see a garden, for example, you can focus in on the entire garden, then focus in on one rosebush, and then further focus in on the bush with one or two more heightened senses. How does it smell? What do the thorns feel like?

take five

Being in the present moment is a key part of mindfulness. Noticing your senses provides you with five ways to step into the present moment. Today think, "Take five," when you do any activity. Notice what you can see, hear, smell, touch, and taste during that activity.

MINDFUL TAKEAWAY

Promote spacious mindful awareness by "taking five" in the activities you are doing today. Spend time focusing on and engaging in activities that nourish and fill you up. Deliberate efforts support directed mindful awareness.

10

JUST BREATHE

Breathing happens whether you pay attention to it or not. You are always breathing, you just might not notice it. Because your breath is always with you, it's a constant that you can choose to notice at any time.

short breathing practice

Notice your breathing right now. Notice through what part of your body (nose or mouth) you bring air in and through what part you release it.

When you first brought attention to your breathing, did it change? Often when you focus on your breathing, it will change and be uncomfortable. It might feel sharp, tight, shallow, or restricted. A helpful illustration of this change is when you are sick and go to see the doctor. A doctor will often ask you to take deep breaths and will use a stethoscope to listen to your breathing. It can be hard to maintain deep breathing like this for too long because you might get light-headed or dizzy. Similarly, when people are first asked to pay attention to their breath and breathing, they change it. This is normal.

Now try to notice your breathing again, this time without changing it. Just tune in to its natural flow in and out. Notice where you breathe in. Do you use your mouth or nose? Notice where you breathe out. Through your mouth or nose? What was that experience like? How was it the same or different from the first short breathing practice?

breathing a grounding focal point

Over time, you will be able to notice your breathing without it changing. Your breathing is another grounding focal point. You can learn what your breathing is like in different emotional and physical states. When something is wrong, your breathing changes. It can be labored, short, shallow, or restricted. Learning to tune in to your breathing can provide you with valuable information about how you are doing emotionally and physically at any given moment.

dropping-in mindfulness practice

Mindfulness is as simple as 1-2-3: notice your (1) body, (2) breath, and (3) mind. You can do this practice anytime you want. This practice is about dropping in to this moment and noticing your body, breath, and mind—both your thoughts and feelings—as each is in the present. It is a practice to check in with yourself. Notice what you feel in your body. Notice what your breath is like as you breathe. Notice what your mind is revealing at this moment. What thoughts or feelings are you noticing? If it helps, you can use some of the suggestions below for each of the three areas of the dropping-in mindfulness practice.

1. YOUR BODY: Scan your body from the tips of your toes, moving up to the top of your head. You can be a detective to what you notice. A new, familiar, painful, or physical sensation might be recognized. There is no need to change anything you notice; it is just about noticing what is present when you notice your body.

2. YOUR BREATH: Take a few seconds and notice your breathing. Perhaps you notice where you bring air in on your next in-breath, through your nose or mouth; then notice where you release air out on your next out-breath, through your nose or mouth. Follow a breath down into your belly; notice your belly rise on the in-breath and gently fall on the out-breath. What do you notice about your breathing?

note: If your breathing changed when you paid attention to it, that is normal and natural. Just notice what the change feels like.

3. YOUR MIND: Notice what is going on in your mind. Take up to a minute and notice what you are thinking and feeling right now.

This practice is about providing you with information on how you are doing at any given moment. Checking in with yourself by doing the dropping-in practice is an accessible and quick way to do so. You can also do the dropping-in practice to drop in to this moment and connect yourself with the present if you are feeling stressed, overwhelmed, caught in your to-do list, and the like.

—— MINDFUL   TAKEAWAY ——

You can check in with how you are doing physically and mentally any time you want by dropping in to the moment and paying attention to your (1) body, (2) breath, and (3) mind.

11

NOTICE YOUR BELLY

Right now, without trying to change it in any way, just notice your breathing. Pay attention to the actual motion of your belly, and notice how it moves when you breathe.

- Notice your stomach rising on the in-breath.

- Notice your stomach falling on the out-breath.

- Notice this for five breaths.

breathing and your body

Expand your awareness beyond your breathing and stomach to your entire body. As you breathe in, oxygen moves into your lungs and is absorbed into the red blood cells in your body. Your breath is also connected to your heart. Your heart rate varies with your breathing. As you breathe in, your heart rate is faster; as you breathe out, it slows down. Your thoughts, feelings, and experiences affect the cadence of your breathing. Your breathing impacts your heart rate and how much oxygen is brought into your body.

breathing and stress

Learning to pay attention to your breathing and finding the natural flow of your breathing can be a great tool to use when you are stressed. Focusing on your breathing can help get you out of your head and stop ruminating on a thought or feeling that distresses you. Your breathing can help connect your mind to the rest of your body. When you direct your attention to your breathing—or if it is easier, to your body—you change your focus away from a stressor. This can be especially helpful with nagging thoughts or difficult emotions.

MINDFUL TAKEAWAY

When you are stressed, notice your breath just as it is. If you are focused on your breathing, you aren't necessarily focusing on whatever is stressing you out.

12

BREATHING AND MOOD

When you make a habit of checking in on your breathing, you learn what is your "normal" or "typical" breathing. At times, you may notice that your breathing feels very different from normal. This difference indicates that something is off physically or emotionally. Your breath can be a red flag, providing you with information you can use to help yourself feel better by adjusting a situation.

counting breaths practice

As you breathe, say to yourself, "Breathing in one, breathing out one; breathing in two, breathing out two." Do this until you get to ten. You can always count breaths when you aren't feeling well physically or emotionally. Counting your breaths can calm you down. It also gives you the opportunity to take a moment or pause long enough so that you can collect yourself and assess what is going on.

Counting breaths can be particularly useful in these circumstances:

- To decrease anxiety and worry

- To reduce anger or frustration

- To calm down

- To make a decision

- To manage stressful situations

MINDFUL TAKEAWAY

When you are stressed, counting breaths can help provide a space between a situation and how you choose to respond to it.

13

YOUR BREATH IS AN ANCHOR TO THIS MOMENT

Think of your chest, and imagine your breathing as an anchor to this moment. You might even want to envision an anchor in your chest area. Your breath can be an anchor, a constant, on which you can focus when you're stressed. It is always with you, and when you notice it, it can ground you and calm you down.

dropping anchor practice

Imagine an anchor that has been dropped into the water to keep a boat moored. As the boat tries to move with the waves, the anchor keeps the boat in place. When you feel like your boat is being pulled adrift by stress, remember your breath is an anchor that can hold you in place and bring you back to the present.

grounding focal points

The following is a list of some potential grounding focal points you can use to anchor yourself when you are stressed:

- Notice the air around your fingers.

- Notice sensations on your hands.

- Grab an ice cube and focus on it melting.

- Walk and notice your feet touching the ground.

- Count your breaths.

- Notice your heartbeat, which is a constant and always with you.

- Notice the connection between your breathing and your heartbeat.

note: When you are just beginning to use these grounding focal points, start with those at the beginning of the list and work your way down. The points at the beginning of the list are easiest for beginners to notice.

You can turn to these grounding focal points when you are feeling out of control, overwhelmed, frustrated, angry, or having other difficult emotions, and need to ground yourself in the moment. They are also helpful to get you out of your head when you can't stop thinking about your to-do list, worrying about the future, or replaying the past.

Can you think of other grounding focal points in your life that can help anchor and drop you down into calm, still waters?

MINDFUL TAKEAWAY

Grounding focal points are constants that are always with you: your fingers, hands, feet, breath, and heartbeat. These points can help keep you anchored in the now, even if you can't change your environment.

14

MINDFULNESS IS ABOUT NOTICING YOUR PHYSICAL SENSATIONS

short body scan practice

Take a minute right now to scan your body from the tips of your toes to the top of your head. Notice what you feel in your body along the way. What do you feel physically? Any aches or pains you hadn't noticed before? What parts of your body feel like they normally do?

After you finish scanning your body, note what position you were in while you did it—sitting, standing, lying down? Each time you do this practice and check in on your body, you will notice something different.

physical cues and red flags

Your body provides you with information about how you are doing both physically and emotionally. Many times, people aren't connected or tuned in to these cues. They may have feelings or thoughts and be in their head, without noticing the red flags from their bodies to alert them that they aren't in physical or mental balance. Here are some physical cues that you are stressed:

- Crying

- Muscle tightness or pain

- Shortness of breath or chest pain

- Stomach ache or nausea

- Sweating or trembling

- Headache

the five ws

Sometimes you know right away what is causing you stress, but there are other times when you have physical cues and don't know why. If you can figure out what is stressing you out, you can try to change it. Go through the five Ws to figure it out.

1. WHO: Who were you with? Were you alone or with others?

2. WHAT: What were you doing right before you felt this way?

3. WHERE: Where were you?

4. WHEN: When did you start to feel this way? What was going on? Explain the situation.

5. WHY: Why might this person, place, thing, or situation be upsetting to you?

Asking yourself these questions can help you figure out what might have triggered your physical cues. A fight? A disappointment? A success or failure? A disagreement?

MINDFUL TAKEAWAY

Check in with your body on a regular basis and consider the five Ws to assess how you are doing. Use this information to make needed changes.

PART TWO

SELF-CARE

Self-Compassion,
Self-Acceptance,
Self-Respect,
Self-Esteem

Part of being mindful is to be
aware of your relationships with yourself
and other people. SELF-CARE
helps you build your resources, get your
needs met, and be for yourself.

Once you have learned some of the foundational practices of mindfulness, you can begin to apply mindfulness to the relationships you have with yourself, others, and the rest of the world.

Compassion, acceptance, respect, and esteem come first from within. You can't truly offer them to others until you have applied them to yourself. You may, for example, be able to partially accept other people and their actions, but unless you have explored self-acceptance, it can be difficult to truly accept others.

This section is about exploring what resources and strengths you possess. When you know what they are, you can use them when you need safety, satisfaction, and connection. This section is about building up your resource bank to enjoy the pleasant aspects of your life, to take in your successes, to manage stress, and to tackle the most difficult moments.

This section also teaches you to do more of what works when things are pleasant and going well and to do something different when things are unpleasant and not working. It teaches you to "be for yourself"— to be a cheerleader for yourself, whether you have a support system or not. It is important to learn to be for yourself.

15

TAKE A BREAK WITH THE THREE Bs

take a mindful pause

It can be helpful and productive to take a *mindful pause*, a break, in certain situations. A mindful pause gives you some space—from a few seconds to hours, whatever is realistically possible—to check in on how you are doing physically and emotionally, and on what feelings or thoughts are coming up for you. This information can help you in many situations in life.

Here are some times it is especially helpful to take a mindful pause (see chapter 39):

- When you are trying to make important decisions

- When you are upset, sad, or angry

- Before starting, or during, a difficult conversation

- Before starting, or during, a project or task

- Before starting, or during, a test or homework

- Before starting, or during, a competitive activity or hobby—sports, music, or dance

take a break with the three Bs

You can always take a short pause, a break, with the three Bs (**B**ody, **B**reathe, **B**egin).

1. BODY: Notice how you feel in your body. Release and relax any tension.

2. BREATHE: Notice your breath. Take a deep breath and follow it from in- to the out-breath.

3. BEGIN: Begin again. Return to whatever you took a pause from, or start anew.

Using the three Bs can help your mood, help you with difficult decisions, and help you before starting, or during, different activities.

MINDFUL TAKEAWAY

Taking a mindful pause creates space in a situation and allows you to respond thoughtfully rather than react impulsively.

16

HAVE YOU EVER WALKED INTO CLASS AND NOT REALIZED HOW YOU GOT THERE?

You can bring mindfulness to walking and every other movement. While you're walking or moving, use your senses (sight, sound, smell, touch, and taste) to guide you in this practice.

mindful walking practice

Walking is something you usually just do, without giving it a lot of thought. Although it often becomes rather automatic, walking presents an opportunity to be open to the various objects of your attention. Where do your thoughts go? What feelings arise?

Your feet, like your breath, are an anchor to the present—an anchor that literally grounds you to the present moment and to the earth. Pay attention to how you walk. Notice what walking feels like in your body: lifting your foot, shifting to the other foot, stepping, and repeating. Try walking on grass with no shoes or socks, if you can. Feel the earth touch your feet. Ground yourself in the moment with every step you take.

When you are emotionally upset, it can be helpful to walk. Take a break, or a mindful pause, and walk when you need space to center yourself again. Make sure you choose a safe place to walk.

mindful movement

Think of different times when you could bring mindful attention to your movements. Mindfulness doesn't require that you do the movement slowly, only that you be present in the movement as you do it. Here are some examples to consider:

- When you are walking around school or work

- When you are walking around your house

- When you dance

- When you play sports or do physical exercise

awareness practice

Mindful awareness is the landscape in which various contents of the mind arise, persist, and pass by. It is a steady attention in the moment, typically with a presence of mind (not lost in thought). In this practice, be mindful of the various objects of your attention:

- Your feet

- Your body

- Your breath

- Your sight—what catches your attention in the landscape around you

- Your mind—thoughts and feelings

mindful walking photography practice

Take a mindful walk with your cell phone or digital camera. While you are walking, take from five to ten pictures of things that catch your eye or interest you. Now make sure to take one picture of something that doesn't quite fit or belong in its current place. Doing this forces you to pay closer attention to your environment. It is often easy to skim over what you see, but when you are focusing in on what doesn't belong, you can often see more.

MINDFUL   TAKEAWAY

All that is important is this one moment in movement. Make the moment vital and worth living. Do not let it slip away unnoticed and unused.
—Martha Graham, a pioneer in modern dance choreography

17

MINDFUL ACTION

Being mindful is paying attention to what you are doing as you are actually doing it.

being mindful of routine activities

Choose a routine activity you do every day—for example, washing dishes, brushing your teeth, taking a shower, or putting on your clothes—and bring mindful attention to it. Notice every aspect of this activity. Considering the following questions will help you do this:

- What are the smaller components, if any, that make up this activity?

- What is the reason you are doing this activity?

- What thoughts are present?

- What feelings or emotions are coming up?

- What are your physical sensations?

- What aspects of this activity can you notice that you have not noticed before?

active versus passive living

You do not have to be a passive participant on automatic pilot. You can choose to act and be present to what you are doing. It is useful to make deliberate efforts, such as reflecting on an experience or paying attention to your senses duing an activity.

Engage your mind to look at experiences in a novel and fresh way. Choose to take in the good. Experience the experience. Feel the feelings. Let the contents in your awareness—the sounds, sights, smells, tastes, touches, and thoughts—come and go without attempting to change them in any way. See what arises. It may surprise you.

MINDFUL TAKEAWAY

Instead of focusing on the negative aspects of doing a chore that you find boring, deliberately notice the good aspects of doing this routine activity.

18

MINDFUL HOBBY: USE INFO

If you live on automatic pilot, you may miss many of life's important moments. You can wake up to your life and be fully aware by bringing moment-to-moment aware-ness to everything you do. Zero in on what you are doing as you are doing it.

being mindful of hobbies

A hobby is an interest or activity you like to do for en-joyment or pleasure—sports, dance, music, playing video games, and so on. You can get into the habit of doing something so routinely that you zone out or are not fully present to what you are doing. Present-moment awareness involves tuning in to your senses (sight, sound, smell, touch, and taste), thoughts, and feelings about what you are doing. With this awareness, you can begin to live your life more fully.

Think of five interests or activities you enjoy. Pick one and do it mindfully. Try to see this hobby with fresh eyes, as if you have never done it before. Being mindful of a hobby can give you renewed interest in something that may have become rather automatic and routine in your life.

The first step is to assess each of your senses while doing the hobby:

- What do you see?

- What do you hear?

- What do you smell?

- What do you touch?

- What do you taste?

The second step is to notice what thoughts or feelings come up for you. These two steps will help you be mindful of the hobby.

use INFO with a hobby

When you are doing a hobby today, be present. Ask yourself these questions and reflect on your answers. Use INFO (**I**nterests, **N**ew, **F**eel, and **O**bserve) to help you.

INTERESTS: What interests you about the hobby?

NEW: Look at the hobby as if it's the first time you have done it. What is new or different about it?

FEEL: What do you feel physically and emotionally when you do things related to this hobby?

OBSERVE: What do you observe in your surroundings?

MINDFUL TAKEAWAY

Consider doing a hobby this week that you haven't done in a while. Apply the INFO questions (Interests, New, Feel, and Observe) while you do your hobby mindfully.

19

MINDFULNESS AND MUSIC

Listen to your favorite song as if it is the first time you have ever heard it.

What did you hear? What was different? What was the same?

music and mood

Music is often tied to your memories. You may remember a song you love because it is tied to some amazing moment in your life, or you may remember a song you strongly dislike because you were in a fight while it was playing. Songs can evoke powerful emotions—both positive and negative. Be mindful of what you are listening to and why you are listening to a particular song or set of songs. If you're depressed, playing music you know brings you down is not in your best interest.

HOT: keep the fire going

Two things are important about campfires: starting the fire and keeping it going. Positive experiences in your life are like campfires. You can have a beneficial experience, but there is extended value when you can keep it going by creating a lasting resource from that experience.

You can use HOT (**H**ave the beneficial experience, **O**pen to the beneficial experience, **T**ake in the beneficial experience) to help turn any good experience into a lasting resource. The following example shows how HOT can be used with music.

Have the beneficial experience. Notice a beneficial experience you are having or go and create one.

example: Listen to one of your favorite songs.

Open to the beneficial experience. Be open to all you can during the experience. Stay with it while it is taking place. Let the experience become more intense. Open to it in your body. Connect how your body feels to your thoughts and feelings. Be present to your senses and to your thoughts and emotions during the experience.

example: If the song has a good beat, move to it. If you know the words, sing to it. Close your eyes and take in the lyrics and music.

Take in the beneficial experience. Let the experience sink into you like water is absorbed into a sponge. Let the experience become part of you.

example: Notice what the lyrics mean to you. Let the enjoyment you feel fill you up. Savor the sweetness. Give yourself permission to enjoy the moment.

MINDFUL TAKEAWAY

Go and do something you enjoy today. Turn your beneficial experience into a lasting resource by using HOT (**H**ave the beneficial experience, **O**pen to the beneficial experience, and **T**ake in the beneficial experience).

20

MINDFUL DOWNTIME

Your body is like a car. It needs fuel to work. You need to refuel and recharge when you are physically or mentally depleted. Taking mindful downtime is a way to refuel and recharge. When you take mindful down time, you are present in the moment and aware of your senses, thoughts, and feelings as you engage in a relaxing or rejuvenating activity.

signs that your physical and emotional gas tank is empty

Knowing when you need physical and mental downtime is important. Here are some red flags that signal you need a break:

- You are irritable, frustrated, sad, and/or angry.

- You are often tired.

- You don't want to do the things you usually enjoy.

- You can't focus.

- You feel overwhelmed.

- You are more emotional than usual.

- You are snappy or short-tempered with other people.

downtime activities to fill up your tank

We are often on the go, but sometimes it is good to just chill out. Doing something that doesn't necessarily require a lot of interaction or mental effort helps. Here are some possible options for downtime activities that can fill you up:

- Watch a movie.

- Read a magazine or book.

- Take a shower or bath.

- Take a nap if you are tired.

- Listen to music that puts you in a good mood.

- Spend time with friends or family.

fundamental needs

The psychologist Rick Hanson says that peoples' fundamental needs are to be safe, to be satisfied, and to feel connected. The following table matches these three fundamental needs with the types of feelings that activate those needs.

Fundamental Need	Feelings That Activate It
Safety or peace	Feeling a pain or threat Feeling vulnerable
Satisfaction or contentment	Experiencing something unpleasant Feeling unhappy, sad, or alone
Connection or love	Feeling a sense of loss Feeling rejected by a nother person

When you are aware of your fundamental needs, you can engage with people, places, things, or situations that support those needs—you can fill up your gas tank and recharge. Consider these questions to assess your own fundamental needs:

SAFETY OR PEACE

- What people, places, things, or situations in your life allow you to feel a sense of safety or peace?

- What people, places, things, or situations lead you to feel vulnerable, unsafe, uncomfortable, pained, or even threatened?

SATISFACTION OR CONTENTMENT

- What people, places, things, or situations do you find pleasant or unpleasant?

- What people, places, things, or situations are you grateful for or happy about?

- What people, places, things, or situations lead you to feel unhappy, sad, or alone?

- What are you satisfied and content with in your life right now?

- What opportunities do you have in your life?

CONNECTION OR LOVE

- Who in your life do you feel a sense of love for or feel loved by?

- Who in your life do you feel connected to?

- Who in your life do you feel disconnected from, uncomfortable with, or rejected by?

- What people, places, things, or situations make you feel a sense of loss or grief?

Asking yourself these questions helps you tune in to the people, places, things, and situations that fill you up and nourish you and those that drain and deplete you. This information can help you seek out people, and spend time doing things, that fill you up when you need to refuel and recharge.

MINDFUL TAKEAWAY

Taking downtime is necessary to be a fully functioning person. Notice the physical and emotional red flags that your gas tank is running low, and fill it up with people, places, things, and situations that nourish and support your fundamental needs for safety, satisfaction, and connection.

21
MINDFUL CALLING

Life today is experienced online, and much face-to-face communication has been replaced by online messages. It is difficult to create, nourish, and grow meaningful connections without seeing people in person, at least some of the time. Without visual contact, you lose the nonverbal communication that can let you know if what you are saying is being well received or even understood. Mistakes, misunderstandings, and misinterpretations can happen.

nonverbal communication is king

Nonverbal communication is the transmission of information to another person without the use of words. It is the single most powerful form of communication. It allows you to interpret the meaning of what someone is saying and doing.

Nonverbal communication provides a lot of information through many channels:

Body language refers to the way people stand; how they sit; how they move their arms, hands, legs, and feet.

Posture describes the way people carry themselves. Are they slumped over or standing tall and upright?

Positioning is the way people place themselves. Are they leaning back comfortably or leaning back to try to get father away from you?

Physical space is the space between you and the person you are communicating with. Are you close or distant?

Gestures punctuate and add meaning to what people are saying. Are they moving their hands up and down for emphasis, fidgeting with a pen, or quickly tapping their feet on the ground?

Touch can convey a person's closeness with you. Does the person pat you on the back, hug you, or hold your hand?

Facial expressions help you figure out people's emotions. What is the position of the mouth (smiling, grimacing)? How do the eyes look (squinting, open wide)? These cues help you assess how someone is feeling angry, happy, hurt, bored, or sad.

Eye contact can be used to convey interest. Is someone looking at you or looking away as you speak?

Nonverbal communication clues you in to what another person is thinking and feeling but may not express in words.

richness of communication

The richest communication is in-person and video real-time communication that enables you to assess someone's intentions, meanings, and feelings through what is said without words. Seeing someone allows you to take in all the different aspects of nonverbal communication.

Although audio-only communication is the second-most valuable form, when you are only able to hear someone, you lose all the information that nonverbal communication provides, except for tone of voice. Aside from actual words people use, their tone of voice—for example, pitch, pacing, loudness, and pauses—conveys useful information about what they intend, mean, and feel.

Real-time communication, or communication that is taking place right now in this moment, is preferable to nonreal-time communication. Nonreal-time communication can be read, viewed, or listened to soon after the fact or at a much later time when it may no longer be relevant.

This list demonstrates forms of communication from the most valuable to least valuable:

- In person, face-to-face

- Face-to-face video

- Audio

- Real-time texts

- Nonreal-time video

- Nonreal-time audio

- Nonreal-time texts

- Nonreal-time e-mails

Several things happen as you move down this scale:

- The value and depth of what you can get from the communication decreases

- The accuracy of the communication decreases

- The potential for misinterpretation increases

It might be more convenient to communicate in non-real time, but you are exchanging value and accuracy for convenience. Instead of texting someone today, see them in person, have a video chat, or give that person a call. Be thoughtful about what you say. Seeing someone and hearing their voice feels a lot different than receiving a text.

What was it like to see someone, video chat, or call instead of texting?

MINDFUL TAKEAWAY

Listen with your eyes during the next in-person conversation you have. Pay attention to all the different areas of the other person's nonverbal communication: body language, posture, positioning, physical space, gestures, touch, facial expression, and eye contact.

22

LOOK UP FROM THE DEVICE

When people are walking, they often are doing a number of other things as well; they may be focused on their phones, tablets, or other electronic devices. There are many life situations in which you are partially attending to a task or person while also attending to a device. You can miss what is happening right in front of you if you are spending a lot of time focused on that device.

the urge to surf social media

The urge to surf on social media can be addictive. One of your brain's neurotransmitters, *dopamine*, is activated while you surf. When something is interesting, new, or novel, more dopamine is released; when it is boring, dopamine goes down. In effect, you get rewarded for spending hours on end browsing different social network pages. You get this dopamine release, this shot of feeling good. Your compulsion to surf is fed by these dopamine hits because you physically want more of it; the message from your brain is, "Give me more."

Furthermore, when you are searching for something, the act of seeking itself releases more dopamine than when you find what you are looking for. You begin to "surf the urge" of wanting more dopamine.

The following are some examples of urge surfing:

- Going to your phone as soon as you wake up in the morning; feeling uncomfortable if you don't do it

- Checking your phone when you aren't supposed to; feeling uncomfortable or like you're missing out if you don't check it

- Checking and then rechecking, almost like an "I have to" feeling

- Striving for numbers on different sites, keeping up a "posting streak" or "watching the likes roll in"

- Being unable to sign off because there is more to look at; feeling like you can't stop or can't turn it off

- Being at an event and finding that posting is more important than enjoying the event itself

- Prioritizing your phone over people right in front of you, so that social media is getting in the way of your life

taking a mindful pause

When you find yourself engaging in any of these behaviors, take a mindful pause. Remember, a mindful pause gives you some space, from a few seconds to hours, to check in with how you are doing physically and emotionally. You can check in on what thoughts or feelings are coming up for you.

riding the urge waves

You may have urges to surf social media, but you don't have to do it. Just because you have an impulse to do something doesn't mean you're forced into it.

- **Notice what the urge feels like.** Ask yourself, "Is there a feeling or need that I'm trying to meet when I follow that urge? Am I trying to avoid something else (procrastinating, denying, or pushing away a difficult feeling)?"

- **Stay curious about your urges.** Tell yourself, "Hmm, interesting. This is what the urge feels like right now." Ask yourself, is it a physical sensation, a mental impulse, or a way to avoid something else in the present?

- **Remember that urge waves will pass.** Like ocean waves that ebb and flow, the urges you have to check and post on social media will pass. Notice what it is like to want to go on your phone and not do it. Don't give in to the urge, and it will eventually subside.

MINDFUL TAKEAWAY

Take a moment now and then to look up from your electronic devices and take in your environment. Consider what you are missing in your surroundings by constantly looking down at your phone or other devices.

23

SELF-CARE

As the well-known columnist Ariana Huffington notes, "We take better care of our smartphones than we do ourselves."

When you take care of yourself, you are saying to yourself that you matter. Engaging in self-care doesn't mean you are selfish. You can't care for anyone else until you first take care of yourself. Then you can model for others how to take care of themselves.

be for yourself

When a phone's battery is almost out of power, the phone will alert you to charge it so it will continue to work. Similarly, when a car is almost out of gas, an icon on the dashboard lights up or flashes, alerting you to the need for fuel. Unlike phones and cars, there is no visual indicator light that tells you when you are depleted or almost empty—physically, mentally, or emotionally.

Being for yourself is a way to help yourself have a

healthy mind and body. Even when others aren't cheering you on or helping you succeed in life, you can be for yourself! One prime way to be for yourself is to engage in self-care.

self-care activities

Self-care is defined as giving attention to your physical and psychological well-being. Self-care activities are positive behaviors or things you do that make you feel good, nourish you, and fill you up. Interestingly, what some people think of as self-care can be quite harmful. If you engage in an activity that harms you physically or mentally (for example, cutting, sexting, binging, or purging), that isn't self-care—it's self-harm.

Here are some examples of positive self-care activities:

- Do something that makes you smile.

- Listen to your favorite (uplifting) music.

- Engage in a hobby you enjoy.

- Spend time with people who build you up, such as friends or family members.

- Take a warm bath or shower.

- Have a nice warm drink, like a cup of tea.

- Spend time looking at or being with nature.

● Eat something healthy.

● Get a restful night's sleep.

● Exercise.

Right now, think about some self-care activities that you do for yourself, and write at least five self-care activities on a piece of paper.

Using A, B, or C from the following list, indicate when you could do each of your activities.

A. Today

B. This week

C. This month

Follow through on performing your self-care activities according to your list.

level I,II,III, and IV self-care activities

Another way to work with self-care activities is to think of how much time it takes you to do each one. You can consider activities that take from one to fifteen minutes as Level I and those that take longer than fifteen minutes—usually a half hour or an hour—as Level II. The idea is to do at least one Level I activity a day and at least one Level II activity a week. Consider activities you like to do when you tell someone you are doing nothing for the day or are taking the day off as Level III. The idea is to take a half to full day off once a month and engage in activities that are on your Level III list. Level IV asks you to take a half to full day, once a month, to spend time with a friend or family member who nourishes and supports you. Of course, you can do more each level, but these are recommendations for starting off.

LEVEL I EXAMPLES

Playing with a pet
Taking a bath or shower
Making a healthy snack
Taking extra time for grooming

LEVEL II EXAMPLES

Taking a nap
Going to a yoga, dance, or exercise class
Reading a book or magazine not related to school
    or work
Going to the movies

LEVEL III EXAMPLES

Salon or spa visit—nail care, massage, facial, haircut
Watch movies or TV
Lie around, nap, sleep
Garden or spend time in nature

LEVEL IV EXAMPLES

Consider people who fill you up and bring you happiness, peace, and joy in the following categories:

Friends
Family
Students
Colleagues

What Level I self-care activity can you do each day this week? What Level II self-care activity can you do once this week? What Level III activities will you do when you have your next day off or down day? Who will you spend time with at least once this month when you do your Level IV self-care? Remember, you can always pick new activities from each of the first three levels; they don't have to be the same each time.

MINDFUL TAKEAWAY

It is important to care for yourself as well as, if not more than, you would care for your smartphone. Practice bringing self-care into your life every day.

24

THE HEART PUMPS BLOOD TO ITSELF FIRST

Taking care of yourself doesn't mean you are selfish. Just think, for the body to work, the heart has to pump blood to itself first before sending it to the rest of the body's organs. You can't effectively care or be there for another person unless you first care for yourself. You can do this by engaging in self-care activities, but first assess if even your most basic of needs are being met.

getting your basic needs met: HALT

When some key needs in your life aren't met, you are more vulnerable to feeling depressed, worried, impulsive, and reactive. The acronym HALT (**H**ungry, **A**ngry, **L**onely, **T**ired) can help you quickly assess whether your immediate needs are being met. Fulfilling these needs allows you to thrive physically and emotionally, and it puts you in a better place to make decisions, function well, and take care of others.

HUNGRY: Have you eaten recently? You might need a snack.

ANGRY: Are you angry at some person, place, thing, or situation? Acknowledge that you're feeling angry; take care of yourself—maybe by taking a mindful pause or a personal time-out.

LONELY: Do you feel lonely? Are you lacking connection with others? Do what you can to engage with another person or a group of people.

TIRED: Have you gotten enough sleep? If not, take a nap or go to bed when you can.

When you are depleted in any of these areas, you are vulnerable to feeling physically poor and/or emotionally off. Paying attention to whether you are hungry, angry, lonely, or tired and addressing these needs when you have them is an important way to take care of yourself and, in turn, take care of others.

your thermostat set point

When you are in balance physically and emotionally—generally feeling "good," "okay," or "well"—you could say that your thermostat is set at just the right temperature: your thermostat set point. Let's say that your temperature is at seventy degrees on the thermostat when you are feeling generally well and balanced. When you get off that set point—for example, you have a fight with your friend—your temperature goes up to ninety-three degrees. When your temperature rises from your balanced set point, your job is to reset it. You can do four things to get yourself back to set point. Use the acronym NAME (**N**otice, **A**ccess, **M**ake, **E**ngage) to help:

NOTICE: Notice when your thermostat is off its set point.

ASSESS: Assess what caused it to be off the set point.

MAKE: Make needed changes and adjustments to return to your set point.

ENGAGE: Engage in the rest of your day.

MINDFUL TAKEAWAY

Even in the worst situations, days, or feelings, you can *always* do something to take care of yourself. Remember to check in on whether you are Hungry, Angry, Lonely, or Tired (HALT) and take care of your basic needs. When your thermostat is off its set point, use NAME to help you Notice, Assess, Make changes, and Engage in the rest of your day.

25

STOP AND SMELL THE ROSES

"Stop and smell the roses" is a tried-and-true adage that reminds people to notice the beauty in the world, the pleasant things that may get missed or passed by. It is useful to make deliberate efforts to pay attention to what you enjoy, what is pleasant to you, and what fills you up physically and emotionally. Taking in the good can help you build up internal resources that support a healthy and well-balanced you.

plant seeds and pull weeds

When you make the effort to (1) notice the good or make the good happen and (2) take in the good, you are growing positive, beneficial, lasting inner resources. It is helpful to plant, cultivate, and grow these positive and beneficial "seeds." They are internal resources you can call on when you are feeling physically and emotionally depleted. It is equally helpful to notice the weeds, those things that drain or deplete you. Plant seeds and pull weeds!

activity: things that nourish and drain you

On a separate piece of paper, list everything you remember doing today, from the minute you woke up until right now. Use a separate line for each item and include everything; nothing is insignificant.

Label the things that nourished you with the letter **N**. They can be anything that helped you thrive physically or emotionally—brushing your teeth, eating, getting a hug from a friend, noticing the sky. Include whatever might have benefited you in some way, even in a miniscule amount.

Now put a **D** next to anything that drained you. This can be anything that negatively impacted or harmed your ability to function physically or emotionally, anything that negatively affected you in some way, no matter how small—a paper cut, someone rolling their eyes at you, being late to class or a meeting, sending an e-mail or text by accident.

There may be some items on your list that you didn't find nourishing or draining. These indifferent or neutral events are normal parts of the day. Just notice these.

Day in and day out, there are going to be things that fill you up and nourish you and things that drain or deplete you. Depending on the day, your mood, and other factors, something you labeled as a drain might at other times nourish you. For example, you just presented a big project and are tired and just feel like being alone. Unexpectedly, two of your friends show up to spend to time with you. In this case, your friends visiting might feel draining to you. However, if you have been working on a project and feel alone and isolated, having your two friends show up to spend time with you might be just the thing that can fill you up and nourish you. Keep in mind that there are many factors that influence and impuct how you see and absorb things on a given day. Consider spending more time on healthy activities and with others who nourish and fill you up, and less time on those who deplete or drain you.

Are you stopping to smell the roses, or are you only noticing the weeds?

Focusing on what fills you up and nourishes you rather than on what drains you takes effort. Consider the areas of your life that sustain and nourish you and those that deplete you. Here are some areas to consider:

- Family

- Friends

- Extracurricular activities and hobbies

When you can build and take in some nourishing resources—a hug from a friend, eating your favorite meal—you will find it easier to manage those things that drain you.

MINDFUL TAKEAWAY

It is beneficial to deliberately take in the good. Stop and smell the roses during your day. Pay attention to something you would normally ignore. Notice the sky, a tree, a flower, a pretty picture. Notice what is cool about something ordinary.

26

THE FIVE Gs

William Arthur Ward, a motivational speaker and author, wrote, "Gratitude can transform common days into thanksgiving, turn routine jobs into joy, and change ordinary opportunities into blessings."

the five Gs

What are five things you are grateful for in your life today? Find a spot where you can sit without electronics or other distractions, and reflect on five things you are thankful to have in your life. During your day, think of someone you are grateful to have in your life and let that person know, preferably by calling or seeing them. If you can't call, text, or e-mail.

four ways to experience and express gratitude

When you are feeling grateful or thankful, you can *experience* or take in gratitude. You can *express* your gratitude outwardly (toward others) or inwardly (toward yourself) by offering thanks. The following table shows four different ways to experience and express gratitude.

Experience Gratitude: Taking It In	Express Gratitude: Letting It Out
1. GRATITUDE TOWARD YOURSELF: You can be grateful for something you have done for yourself or another person. You can acknowledge what you have done for yourself or another person.	You can thank yourself.
2. GRATITUDE TOWARD SOMEONE ELSE: You can be grateful when someone else does something for you—a favor or gesture.	You can thank someone for a favor or gesture.
3. GRATITUDE TOWARD YOURSELF FOR A GIFT: You can be grateful when you buy a gift for yourself. You can acknowledge the gift you bought yourself.	You can thank yourself for the gift you bought yourself. You can consider your act of self-generosity.
4. GRATITUDE TOWARD SOMEONE ELSE FOR A GIFT: You can be grateful when you receive a gift from another person. You can acknowledge the gift received from another person.	You can thank someone for a gift. You can thank someone for an act of generosity.

the power in saying thank you

Recognizing that you want to thank someone requires some effort on your part, and you have the power to choose to express your gratitude or not. It can be very powerful to say "thank you" for something someone has done for you. These words can have particular impact when the person isn't expecting to be thanked and/or really needs to hear those words. Pay attention to peoples' responses when you thank them. Also pay attention to how you feel when you express your thanks.

How often do you take the time to mentally say "thank you" to yourself? At first, you might think this would be corny, weird, or awkward. But why is it any less important to thank yourself than it is to thank someone else? Over the next week, thank yourself once a day.

Here are a few things you can thank yourself for:

- Being who you are right now in this moment

- Something you have done for yourself

- Something you have done for another person

- Your strengths, gifts, or talents

Notice what it feels like when you take the time to acknowledge yourself by giving thanks.

MINDFUL TAKEAWAY

When you wake up and before you go to sleep, think about five things you are grateful for. Doing this will often improve your mood.

27

AN ATTITUDE OF GRATITUDE

The author and activist Elie Wiesel wrote, "When a person doesn't have gratitude, something is missing in his or her humanity. A person can almost be defined by his or her own attitude toward gratitude."

Right now, stop and ask yourself, "What am I grateful for?" If you can't think of anything, ask yourself, "Is there any part of my health, family, friends, pets, school, work, or hobbies that I am grateful for?"

gratitude and your needs

As a human being, your three fundamental needs are to feel safe, satisfied, and connected. When one or more of these needs aren't being met, your brain is alerted to this. For example, if you have been alone all day in your house, you might feel a lack of connection. You go spend time with friends or family, and then you feel connected again. As another example, it isn't until you are sick that you realize just how grateful you are for your health. Once you recover, that sense of satisfaction and contentment from feeling better often passes quickly. In these examples, it isn't until something you need is missing that the realization of what you had is activated. (See chapter 20 for a more thorough breakdown of your fundamental needs.)

fundamental needs assesment: ARGR

It can be useful to evaluate and assess what fundamentals are being met to keep you safe, satisfied, and connected. You can do this by using the acronym ARGR (**A**ttention, **R**eflection, **G**ratitude, and **R**outine).

ATTENTION: Pay attention to which of your fundamental needs are being met right now: safety, satisfaction, and/or connection.

REFLECTION: Reflect on and take in feeling safe, satisfied, and/or connected at this moment in time. Keep any of these beneficial thoughts or feelings with you for the rest of the day.

GRATITUDE: Be grateful for your safety, satisfaction, and/or connection. Acknowledge what parts of your life are working right instead of focusing on what isn't going well.

ROUTINE: Get into a routine of going through this needs assessment every day. Be grateful when even your most basic needs are being met. By doing so, you start building your gratitude muscles. Feeling grateful can improve your physical and mental health.

you are fundamentally okay right now

At any given moment, there is more right with you than there is wrong. That might be hard to believe when you are having a terrible day, week, or even month. To protect you from harm, your brain is biologically wired to attend to whatever isn't working right, to anything that is bad or negative. This is called the brain's *negative selection bias*.

It is so much more important to pay attention to what is working and to what you are grateful for, because it compensates for your brain's overemphasis on the negative. Think about some of the resources you have that enable you to be okay right now. You can consider the following questions:

- Can you see?

- Can you hear?

- Can you drink clean water?

- Can you breathe clean air?

- Can you eat when you are hungry?

- What luxuries do you have—electricity, a roof over your head, warm clothes?

This list captures resources you may have that can go unnoticed because they are such fundamental parts of your daily life. Acknowledging your resources doesn't mean you don't have miserable days, bad things don't happen, or you'll never feel awful. It also doesn't mean there aren't times when some of these resources aren't available to you. Acknowledging what resources you do have means that more often than not there is much more right with you than there is wrong. Remember that it is important to focus on what you are grateful for to help offset your brain's inborn difficulty in taking in good experiences.

MINDFUL   TAKEAWAY

There is more right with you than there is wrong at any given moment. Consider your fundamental needs—safety, satisfaction, and connection—and be grateful for those needs that are being met right now. Remember to bring an attitude of gratitude to your day!

28

MINDFUL ACCEPTANCE

"It is what it is." This is one way to sum up the essence of acceptance—the ability to accept a person, place, thing, or situation as it is in the moment. Acceptance is not necessarily easy, but when you can learn to accept things the way they are, especially those that are out of your control, the result is often feeling like a weight has been lifted off your back.

mindful acceptance: PAC

To mindfully accept what is going on in your life, consider PAC (be **P**resent, take **A**ction, and consider **C**ontrol):

BE PRESENT: Notice and take an inventory of the people, places, things, and situations in your life right now. Being present and aware of these will provide you with information.

TAKE ACTION: Decide if what you are accepting requires any action on your part. If it does, take the necessary action. For example, you might not like the wage you are being paid to work. You accept that this is what you are being paid. If you don't think it is a fair wage, or if you want to be paid more, you can take action. You can go and look for another job that pays more. You can talk to your boss about your wants and needs regarding your wage. When you are accepting of things as the way they are, it doesn't mean you don't want something different. You can take action to change the things you can.

CONSIDER CONTROL: Do you have any control over what is taking place, or is it out of your control? If it is within your control, do what you can and need to, perhaps by choosing to take action. If it is out of your control, be present to whatever thoughts and feelings arise.

You are practicing mindful acceptance when you are present to what is taking place in your life and surroundings. You can decide if anything requires action on your part, and you can recognize what is and isn't within your control.

acceptance inventory

It is often easy to accept things when they are good and going your way. However, it can be difficult to accept things you don't like, things you wish could be different, or things that are out of your control. Mindful acceptance is being present to both the good and the bad. Reflect on each of the following areas:

- **Acceptance of what exists in this moment in your life**
  example: I am sitting at home having a cup of tea while listening to my dog bark at the door.

- **Acceptance of what is within your control**
  example: I can decide when I do my work and when I take a break.

- **Acceptance of what is out of your control**
  example: I have no control of who likes or doesn't like me.

- **Acceptance of your strengths and positive qualities**
  example: I am good at picking new music on iTunes.

- **Acceptance of your flaws and weaknesses**
  example: I am not good at setting limits around how late I stay up at night.

- **Acceptance of what is pleasant to you**
  example: I am enjoying the flower arrangement in front of me.

- **Acceptance of what is unpleasant to you**
  example: I am not as far along with my work as I would like to be.

What you identify for each of these areas will change depending on your mood, the kind of day you are having, your circumstances, and the events in your life.

MINDFUL TAKEAWAY

Accepting who you are and what is going on in your life right now can help you feel more content, at ease, and peaceful. Flaws shape who you are. Can you accept some of your unique qualities that you consider to be flaws? Instead of being mean, harsh, or beating yourself up, can you be gentle, compassionate, and kind toward your flaws?

29

HEARTFULNESS: SHARING KIND THOUGHTS

In Chinese, the characters for *mind* and *heart* are the same, so mindfulness could also be called heartfulness. Heartfulness is a practice that can be used to send warm wishes, kind regards, and kind thoughts to the world, to another person, and to yourself. When you are feeling miserable, frustrated, worried, scared, or overwhelmed, or when things just aren't going your way, it is often a good time to do this practice. It is in these times, when things aren't good, that the heartfulness practice can help.

get ready for the heartfulness practice

1. Sit somewhere quiet, preferably without electronics or other distractions.

2. Gently close your eyes if you are comfortable doing so.

3. Get into a comfortable position.

4. Scan your body from the tips of your toes to the top of your head, just checking in on how your body feels.

5. Notice your breath. Count a few breaths and say, "Breathing in one, breathing out one. Breathing in two, breathing out two." Continue to count in this way until you start to feel a little more settled in.

6. Silently read the following practice to yourself. You can repeat each verse twice or read the entire practice through once and then repeat it.

heartfulness practice

Say the following silently and direct it at the world:

May all people be peaceful.
May all people be happy.
May all people be healthy.
May all people be filled with heartfulness.

Say the following silently and direct it at another person:

May you be peaceful.
May you be happy.
May you be healthy.
May you be filled with heartfulness.

Say the following silently and direct it to yourself:

May I be peaceful.
May I be happy.
May I be healthy.
May I be filled with heartfulness.

Close the heartfulness practice by thanking yourself for the opportunity to offer the world, another person, and yourself these kind wishes and warm regards.

heartfulness 2.0 practice

You can choose phrases and words in your heartfulness practice that resonate with you. Deatrice Anderson, a youth advocate and community educator, shared some alternative language for a heartfulness practice. Her practice has been adapted here to create a newer, less traditional heartfulness practice, called Heartfulness 2.0. The practice follows here.

Say the following silently and direct it at the world:

May all people be happy.
May all people be safe and free from inner
*   and outer harm.*
May all people be surrounded by truth and
*   love forever and always.*
May all people live in peace.
May all people be filled with heartfulness.

Say the following silently and direct it at another person:

> *May you be happy.*
> *May you be safe and free from inner and outer harm.*
> *May you be surrounded by truth and love forever and always.*
> *May you live in peace.*
> *May you be filled with heartfulness.*

Say the following silently and direct it to yourself:

> *May I be happy.*
> *May I be safe and free from inner and outer harm.*
> *May I be surrounded by truth and love forever and always.*
> *May I live in peace.*
> *May I be filled with heartfulness.*

Close this Heartfulness 2.0 practice by thanking yourself for the opportunity to offer the world, another person, and yourself these kind wishes and warm regards.

MINDFUL   TAKEAWAY

Heartfulness is sharing warm wishes, kind regards, and kind thoughts, about others or yourself. Send someone, including yourself, kind thoughts.

30

BE KIND TO YOURSELF

The playwright and novelist Oscar Wilde wrote, "Be yourself; everyone else is already taken."

Give yourself permission to always be kind to your self. This isn't necessarily easy, but you can *choose* to be gentle toward yourself, especially when you have done something you wish you hadn't. When you feel miserable and wish you were feeling better. Or even when you wanted to get something done and didn't.

Can you give yourself permission to be kind and gentle toward yourself, even in the face of difficult circumstances? When you start an inner dialogue of negativity—being mean to yourself or beating yourself up with judgments—or you begin to hear your inner self-critic tearing you down, ask yourself another question: "Would I speak to one of my best friends like this?" The answer is usually no. Of course you are not going to verbally attack and criticize your friends. They probably wouldn't stay your friends for long if you did.

pulling teeth to notice strengths

Right now, take some time and think of five strengths or positive qualities you have. Try to remember them throughout the day today. Sometimes it can be difficult to notice your own strengths. Most often, people can quickly rattle off their weaknesses, flaws, and supposed negative qualities. But when asked what their strengths are, the response can be slow. You don't have to feel guilty or bad about having or acknowledging your strengths, or for thinking positively about yourself. If you decide to share and discuss these positive qualities and strengths with someone, it is important that you choose someone who supports you and makes you feel safe. Consider sharing some of your positive strengths and qualities with someone who genuinely cheers you on!

self-compassion

Self-compassion is a commitment to turn toward your heart and bring love to all the parts of yourself, even the painful parts—physical and mental. Open your heart by connecting with other people, nature, your senses, your feelings, and the world around you. Doing this deepens your self-compassion. Rather than an action or something you have to do outwardly, self-compassion is an attitude you bring to yourself. It is acknowledging and letting yourself know that you matter.

SELF-COMPASSION PRACTICE

People often create and bring pain and suffering into

their lives and relationships. You have the choice of where to focus your attention. Instead of focusing on a painful situation, bring compassion in. Consider a person, place, thing, or situation that is causing you pain, suffering, discomfort, or difficulty, then choose to follow these steps:

STEP 1. Acknowledge your painful situation.

example: Acknowledge that you lied to someone you care about.

STEP 2. Recognize your situation as being part of the normal human condition.

example: Recognize that although you wish you hadn't lied, you did, and it is part of the normal human experience.

STEP 3. Have the desire and wish not to suffer.

example: Have the desire that the suffering you feel because you lied will end.

STEP 4. Bring kindness into your heart.

example: Even though you lied and did something you wish you hadn't, recognize it, you can still bring kindness, love, positive concern, and warm wishes to yourself and into your heart.

STEP 5. Have compassion for your situation.

example: Be compassionate with what happened. You can choose not to lie in the future.

MINDFUL TAKEAWAY

Even at times when you can't relieve your pain or suffering, sincere self-compassion—being kind to yourself—can make things better. Research shows that having self-compassion makes people stronger, more secure, steadier, and more responsive.

31

POSITIVE AND NEGATIVE SELF-TALK

People often don't take in and let their positive self talk stick; conversely, they can't let go of their negative self-talk. Think of three positive qualities you have. What does it feel like to notice your positive qualities? Think of three negative qualities you have. What does it feel like to notice your negative qualities? When you notice negative qualities, remember and silently repeat those three positive qualities to yourself.

positive self-talk: kindling for your fire

Earlier in the book the acronym HOT described a way to take a beneficial experience and create a lasting resource from it. HOT means Having a beneficial experience, Opening to it, and Taking It in. To keep a campfire going, you need to maintain it by adding wood, newspaper, or some sort of kindling. Positive self-talk is the kindling to keep your own fire going and combat negative self-talk, which is the water that puts your fire out.

take in the good and wash out the bad

Research shows that positive self-talk, thinking, and actions can wash through your brain and get rid of your "stuckness." You can shift your mind away from negative self-talk and change yucky feelings about yourself to more positive upbeat ones. It takes deliberate effort to have and recognize positive thoughts and take them in. You can fight the natural tendency to focus on your negative qualities by considering your positive qualities, resources, and strengths:

- A positive quality about yourself

- A talent or ability you have

- A basic need you have that keeps you safe
  (for example, shelter, food, water, air, clothes)

- People who are your friends

- People who support or keep you safe

When you consider any of these positive qualities, resources, and strengths, you can take in the good from them. Doing this allows you to recharge and refuel. Noticing these helps you manage stress and deal with life's challenges.

MINDFUL TAKEAWAY

The psychologist Rick Hanson writes, "We are Velcro to the negative and Teflon to the positive." On a separate sheet of paper, write down your perceived negative and positive qualities by using facts. When using facts, which list is longer? Use the tools in this book to start being Velcro to the positive and Teflon to the negative.

32

KIND ACTS TO ANOTHER

The cartoonist Scott Adams wrote, "Remember there's no such thing as a small act of kindness. Every act creates a ripple with no logical end."

In chapter 29, you read about heartfulness, the practice of sending kind *thoughts* to the world, another person, and yourself. This chapter is about kind *acts* and focuses on doing something positive for someone else.

acts of kindness

Acts of kindness are done on purpose and for a specific reason—to show support, compassion, and caring to another person in some way. These acts take into consideration what the other person's needs or wants might be. There are many ways to offer kindness. Look at the following list for some ideas:

- **Give a gift that you purchase or can get for free.**
  examples:
  You pick a wildflower and give it to a friend who loves flowers.

  You buy your best friend lunch because he forgot his wallet at home.

  You give your mom a candle because she hasn't been feeling well, and you want to brighten her day.

- **Do a favor for someone else.**
  examples:
  You give a lift to someone who needs a ride because his car won't start.

  You let someone borrow your phone because hers needs charging.

  You copy your notes from a meeting and give it to a friend who is home sick.

- **Say something kind to another person.**
  examples:
  Tell someone how important she is to you, using specific examples.

  Compliment someone.

  Acknowledge a person by saying hello and inquire about his day.

- **Offer a kind nonverbal gesture to another person.**
  examples:
  Give someone who is crying a tissue.

  Hug someone you care about.

  Smile at someone you appreciate having in your life.

When you offer kind acts to people, notice how they respond both nonverbally and verbally. Notice their face (lips and eyes), and listen to what they say to you in response. Check in with yourself and notice how it felt to offer kindness to another person, no matter how small the act was. What was it like to do something to brighten someone's day and to be kind to someone else?

random acts of kindness

Diana, Princess of Wales, once said, "Carry out a random act of kindness, with no expectation of reward, safe in the knowledge that one day someone might do the same for you." A random act of kindness is a selfless act done to help cheer someone up or make someone happy. This person could be someone you know or a total stranger. You might choose to do a random act of kindness and not even tell someone you did it. Here are some examples of random acts of kindness:

- Pay for lunch for someone in line behind you without telling them.

- Place a flower on a friend's doorstep.

- Give out at least one compliment a day.

- At a restaurant, if your server does a good job, let his manager know.

The Random Acts of Kindness Foundation shares the scientifically proven benefits of being kind. Check out what kindness can do for you:

Kindness Increases	Kindness Decreases
Energy	Pain
Happiness	Stress
Life span	Anxiety
Pleasure	Depression
Serotonin (a type of chemical neurotransmitter in the body that maintains mood balance)	Blood pressure

MINDFUL   TAKEAWAY

The positive effects of doing acts of kindness are immeasurable. Do or say something nice to someone else today for no reason. Notice what it feels like when you are kind to another person.

33

BE PRESENT TO OTHERS

The author and educator Parker Palmer wrote, "Here's the deal. The human doesn't want to be advised or fixed or saved. It simply wants to be witnessed—to be seen, heard, and companioned exactly as it is."

In the next conversation you have, listen to the person and try not to think of the next thing you're going to say. Let them know what you think you heard them say.

give the gift of presence

People want to be seen and heard. Instead of giving others presents, give them your presence. Giving your full attention to another person can be an amazing gift.

Do you attend to other peoples' needs and wants and forget about your own? You can also give yourself the gift of your presence. Be present to your own wants and needs too.

The following list offers ten ways you can give the gift of presence to others and yourself:

1. Be in the now. Practice mindfulness. Notice your grounding focal points. Notice your five senses. Check in with what you are thinking and feeling. Open to your environment. Be present to other people and let them know you see and hear them. Be present to yourself too.

2. Actively listen. Listen to your gut and your intuition. Give your full attention to someone else or yourself by minimizing other distractions—phone, the Internet, and so on. Use multiple forms of verbal and nonverbal communication (eyes, body language, nods when appropriate) to let others know you are listening.

3. Honor needs. Be present to your needs. Notice when you are **H**ungry, **A**ngry, **L**onely, or **T**ired (HALT). Teach other people HALT so they can honor their own needs.

4. Engage in self-care. Engage in a positive activity that will fill you up and nourish you. Teach others that it isn't selfish to take care of themselves.

5. Allow time for play. Spend time having fun by yourself or with someone else. Play in the snow or the rain, listen to and sing along with some music, enjoy the process of decorating your room. There are many ways to have good, old-fashioned fun.

6. Do for others. Reflect on how you would like to be treated or the things you wish others would do for you. Do them for another person or yourself.

7. Focus on strengths. Acknowledge your own strengths when you see them in action. When you see strengths in others, let them know it.

8. Practice kindness. Today, do one kind act for another person that doesn't get you anything in return. Do one kind act for yourself today.

9. Take a break from social media. Focus on others and yourself without the use of social media. Communicate with others through a call, a text, or a face-to-face visit. Turn off social media for an entire day.

10. Take in the good. Alone or with someone else, engage in what you consider a positive and healthy experience. Take time to practice HOT (**H**ave the beneficial experience. **O**pen to the beneficial experience. **T**ake in the beneficial experience).

Try any of these ten ways to be present every day, once a week, or once a month. When you are aware of engaging in any of these gifts of presence, notice what it feels like, savor it, and take it in.

MINDFUL TAKEAWAY

Thich Nhat Hanh, a well-known peace activist and Zen master, said, "The most precious gift we can offer others is our presence. When mindfulness embraces those we love, they will bloom like flowers." Take the time to be present for yourself and another person today. Notice how it feels when you do this.

PART THREE

ACORN

Always Consider Other Responses Now

Each moment you have the choice of how you want to feel, what you want to think, and how you want to respond. ACORN helps you get out of feeling stuck with your thoughts and feelings and provides you with the skills to live in the now.

Author, psychiatrist, and Holocaust survivor Viktor Frankl wrote, "Between stimulus and response there is a space. In that space is our power to choose our response. In our response lies our growth and our freedom."

It is hard sometimes to realize that you have power, control, and agency over your life, but you do. You can't control what other people do, and you don't have control over some of the decisions others make for you. However, you do have control over how you think, how you feel, and how you choose to respond to every life situation.

This section provides you with many mindfulness-based skills to effectively handle and manage life situations as they present themselves. There will be many times in your life when you will try to assess a person, place, thing, or situation; to make sense of it; and finally to decide what to do if action is required. ACORN (**A**lways **C**onsider **O**ther **R**esponses **N**ow) gives you the tools to assess, understand, and make thoughtful responses or actions.

34

RIDING THE WAVE

Jon Kabat-Zinn wrote, "You can't stop the waves, but you can learn to surf."

Stress can be viewed as waves in the ocean. many stressors, many waves; few stressors, few waves. Just as you can't stop waves, you can't stop stress from coming, but what you do with the stress, how you handle it, will impact how much it affects you. Learning to surf over literal waves is one way to manage them, but how can you manage your stress waves? Most of the skills laid out in this book are meant to guide you through that process.

anchoring your stress waves

What stressors make up your stress waves right now? Imagine being on a rowboat in the ocean. The waves around you represent everything that is stressful for you. Consider the people, places, things, and situations that are causing you stress. Are your waves calm and still, or do they feel as if they're overwhelming, like a big tsunami? Calm waters represent little stress, and large waves indicate a lot of stress. What are your stress waves like right now?

Imagine that you drop an anchor into the water. The anchor will keep your rowboat from drifting away into your stressors. Down deep in the ocean, the water is calm, peaceful, and still. Even during the strongest of storms with huge, crashing waves, the water is perfectly calm deep below the surface. Using your breath is like dropping an anchor into the ocean; it can help you get to your still waters. All of the grounding focal points can help anchor you.

impermanence of waves

Like waves changing, stressors and how stressed you are can change vastly from day to day. Sometimes it is easier to ride the waves when you remind yourself that things change and are impermanent. *Impermanence* means that things don't stay the same forever; everything is temporary and fleeting. Remember that no matter what the issue, how it will affect you depends on many factors, such as your current mood, what you are thinking, and even what you ate for breakfast. What is important to you right now may very well not be important to you later on. Knowing that things will change can sometimes help you tolerate what can feel like an intolerable situation.

MINDFUL TAKEAWAY

When you are caught in the waves—stressors—of life, remember to use your grounding focal points (for example, fingers, hands, feet, breathing, heartbeat) to anchor you to the calm stillness deep below the surface of the water.

35

GOOD DAY, BAD DAY

According to the Olympic gymnast Aly Raisman, "You have to remember that the hard days are what make you stronger. The bad days make you realize what a good day is. If you never had any bad days, you would never have that sense of accomplishment!"

At the ends of most days, many people think back on whether their day was good or bad, defining it as a whole. In truth, their day was most likely a mixture of good and bad moments, not one or the other.

life moments

To process information quickly, your brain assesses and categorizes whether something is good/safe or bad/unsafe. It is normal and natural to categorize things in this way to allow you to move through your day at a regular pace. However, because of this quick categorization, you can end up judging your day as "all good" or "all bad," when, in reality, it is composed of many different life moments—some good, some bad, and some neutral.

consider: PUN

All the hours of your day are filled with life moments—all the things you did, from getting out of bed in the morning to your head hitting the pillow at night. Use a separate piece of paper and write down, one item per line, all the things you remember doing today. Use PUN (**P**leasant, **U**npleasant, and **N**eutral) to help assess your life moments. Next to each item, write **P** for those moments that you consider pleasant or good, **U** for those that were unpleasant or bad, and **N** for those that were neutral, neither pleasant or unpleasant. How much of your day was spent in each of these categories? What thoughts or feelings are present for you as you reflect on your day?

There are two interesting things to consider when reflecting on how your day has gone. First, even when there was something pleasant, ask yourself if there was a sliver of something unpleasant going on at the same time. Conversely, if something unpleasant happened, think about whether there was also something a little pleasant at the same time. Second, can you now begin to consider that a moment can be both good and bad at the same time? Can you think of a moment from your day today that was both pleasant and unpleasant?

attachment to the pleasant

There are times when something is so enjoyable or feels so good that you "attach" to that moment and do not want it to pass. It is healthy to enjoy and savor the sweetness, but it can become harmful if you cling to the moment so tightly that you start worrying about when it is going to be over or stressing that it is ending. For example, have you ever been enjoying a Sunday and then realized that your weekend is quickly coming to an end and you have to go to school or work tomorrow? This type of realization can often change your mood and your experience of whatever you are doing in that particular moment. It can even change your outlook for the rest of the day.

The point is to savor sweet and pleasant moments without worrying about what's going to happen next. Try not to cling to the moment you are in, because it is going to pass. All life moments are impermanent.

MINDFUL TAKEAWAY

People often categorize their day as being either good or bad. Even on a "bad" day, something pleasant usually happens. Pay attention to pleasant things in your day today. Notice the moments that bring you happiness, peace, and joy. Try not to focus on the negative. Remember that whether the moment is pleasant, unpleasant, or neutral, it will pass.

36

PAST, NOW, FUTURE

Are you really here right now? You might think so, but even if you are physically present, your mind may be somewhere totally different. Often when you are thinking, your thoughts are about something that has already happened or about things that are going to happen. When you are thinking about the past or the future, you aren't living in the now.

living in the past or future

It's normal to think about the past; remembering it can help you make decisions about something you are going to do. It is also normal to think about and plan for the future. What becomes particularly unhelpful or harmful is focusing on past or future thoughts that affect you negatively. For example, negative past thoughts often involve ruminating about how something went or judging how you did something. Negative future thoughts often involve worrying about how something you have no control over is going to turn out. Negative past and future thoughts can be harmful as they generally involve the following:

- Judging

- Worrying

- Rehearsing

- Ruminating

- Catastrophizing

past-now-future activity

For two minutes, write down on a piece of paper what you are thinking about. Use one line for each thought. Now go back and label each thought. Use a **P** for any thought that was about the past, an **N** for any thought that was about the "now" (the present), and an **F** for any thought that was about the future. Tally them up. How many of your thoughts were in the now? Most people report that many of their thoughts are **P**s or **F**s, but there are few **N**s. You may be living in the past or future and missing out on your life right *now*!

the landscape of your thoughts

Noticing the landscape of your thoughts can be very useful. Why does this matter? If many of your thoughts are worrisome, painful, and judgmental, they can harm you physically and emotionally. Thinking in this way can also skew your viewpoint toward the negative. When you are focused on negative thoughts, it is like stepping on a piece of gum; it sticks with you and picks up more debris, or negative thinking. If you notice that your thoughts are so strongly focused on the past and/or future that you can't stop thinking about it/them, you can make a change to be in the NOW (Notice, Open and observe, and Ws):

1. NOTICE: Notice the thoughts you're having. Are you focusing on the past, the future, or a combination of the two?

2. OPEN AND OBSERVE: Open to the idea of moving on and thinking about a different topic. Choose to have a new thought that is about something in the now. Observe the present. What is around you right now? Use your five senses to notice what you see, hear, smell, touch, and/or taste right now. This brings you into the now and makes you present in your environment.

3. Ws: WHO, WHAT, WHERE, WHEN, AND WHY?: Ask yourself about your situation at this moment. Who is with you? What are you doing? Where are you? When are you going to do something else? Why do you stay with this activity? Answering these informational questions brings you into the present, to what is occurring in your life right now. If you find that what you're doing is causing you to focus on negative past or future thoughts, do something different. If you can't change the people, place, thing, or situation, focus on using your grounding focal points. Remember that these points are constants that are always with you: your fingers, hands, feet, breath, and heartbeat. These grounding anchors can help keep you centered in the now, even if you can't change your environment.

MINDFUL TAKEAWAY

If you catch yourself thinking negatively about the past or future, direct yourself to something in the now. Start living in the NOW instead of reliving the past or worrying about the future.

37

DON'T BELIEVE
EVERYTHING YOU THINK

Just because you think something, it doesn't mean it's true or real. What are some of the thoughts you are having right now? Are they true and real, or fake and judgmental? Sometimes it can be difficult to accurately assess whether what you are thinking is the truth.

about thoughts

When you are evaluating what you think about another person, place, thing, or situation and deciding how you want to respond or what decision you want to take, reflect on the following:

- A thought is just a thought.

- You don't have to believe your thought.

- You don't have to give power or life to a thought.

- A thought may not be true, real, or factual.

- Sometimes the first thought that comes to your mind can be wrong.

STOP before you act on a thought

Before you respond, make a decision, or act on a thought, use the acronym STOP (**S**top right now, **T**ake a breath, **O**pen and observe, **P**roceed). Using STOP can help you decrease the automatic impulse to react and can allow you to respond more thoughtfully.

STOP RIGHT NOW: Stop and notice the thought you are having at this moment. Is this thought true, real, and factual? If you don't know, find out. Make more sense of it before proceeding.

TAKE A BREATH: Take a breath before making a decision or taking any action. Just sit with the thought while you notice your breathing. Is your breathing normal for you, or is it shallow, tight, or restricted? If it is shallow, tight, or restricted, pause before you respond to someone else, make a decision, or act on your thought. Until your breathing is in the range of what you consider normal, don't continue on your current path.

OPEN AND OBSERVE: Open and observe what you are thinking and feeling right now. Open to your heart and heart-space. Check in with your feelings. If you are experiencing sadness, anger, frustration, anxiety, or other difficult emotions, observe them. Notice why you're feeling that way right now. If you open to your heart and you feel happy, joyful, content, or peaceful, notice why you're feeling that way right now.

PROCEED: Before you move forward, use what you learned by stopping, taking a breath, and opening and observing to decide whether you are:

- On the right train of thought (it isn't harming you in any way to continue thinking about what you're thinking about)

- In a good place to make a decision

- In the right frame of mind to respond to or take action in a given situation

If, during your STOP assessment, you experience difficult breathing or feelings, let these observations guide what you do next. You can always take a mindful pause and then proceed.

MINDFUL TAKEAWAY

Before you believe what you think, ask yourself if it is true, real, and factual. Just because you think something, it doesn't mean you have to believe it or act on it. You can always use STOP (**Stop right now, Take** a breath, **Open** and observe, and **Pro-ceed**) to decide whether to act on your thoughts.

38

MINDFULNESS IS ABOUT NOTICING YOUR THOUGHTS

The neuropsychologist Donald Hebb said, "Neurons that fire together wire together." This means that when two brain neurons connect, or "fire together," their connection or wiring strengthens. It then becomes easier for them to get a response from a third neuron, creating strong neural networks. Every experience, thought, feeling, and sensation triggers neurons to fire and wire together. You may be wondering what neurons, wiring, and your brain's neurochemistry have to do with mindfulness and noticing your thoughts. Keep reading!

your brain in action

Your brain is constantly changing, creating new neurons and making new neural connections. These connections allow you to learn, store, and recall information. For example, neural networks help you remember the name of a person you just met. Neural connections also help you make decisions and complete tasks. For example, when you repeat an experience, like getting dressed each day or taking a walk, your brain learns to trigger the same neurons each time so you can remember how to get dressed or walk.

the bad news: negative begets more negative

Your neural networks can connect negatively and even be harmful to you when you perceive people, places, things, or situations as bad. For example, let's say someone has a bad experience in a romantic relationship. He then thinks he will have the same fate in all future romantic relationships. This can limit him from getting into or staying in romantic relationships. Of course, it is possible that a future relationship will be negative, but it is not necessarily so. Think about another example: a student who is bored by a certain class at school gets a bad grade and is shamed by the teacher. This student then begins to see academics as a whole as something negative. This neural connection can limit her in many ways. For example, she could stop putting effort in her other classes and choose a class load next year that is beneath her ability. Bad experiences can turn into negative imprints on the brain, but they don't have to.

the good news: neuroplasticity

Neuroplasticity is the ability of the brain to change by creating and reorganizing neural connections, especially in response to learning or experience. Depending on how it is used, the brain can grow approximately fourteen hundred new neurons a day and can create a myriad of new neural connections. The brain changes in response to experience, particularly with positive or pleasurable experiences. By tilting toward the positive, you help positive neural connections grow. That is why it is so important to do the following to help tilt toward the positive:

- **Take in the good.** Use the acronym HOT (**H**ave a beneficial experience, **O**bserve the beneficial experience, and **T**ake in the beneficial experience) to help you create lasting resources.

- **Plant seeds and pull weeds.** Do more of what nourishes you and fills you up and less of what depletes and drains you.

- **Take care of yourself.** Be for yourself. Engage in Level I, II, and III self-care activities and spend time with healthy people, Level IV.

mindfulness: be aware of your thoughts

You have many thoughts all the time. It is what you do with those thoughts—the decisions you make, and the actions you take—that determines how they impact you. When you are mindful of your thoughts, you are aware of them. Awareness is king. Mindful awareness can be both spacious and directed. You can be *spaciously* aware of your senses, surroundings, thoughts, and feelings. Once you become spaciously aware, you can then deliberately *direct* your attention. You can choose to direct your attention to things that fill you up or nourish you and on taking in the good. You can move away from automatic reacting to thoughtfully responding.

What are you thinking about right now? Spend the next thirty seconds noticing your thoughts. What did you think about? Was there anything new or different that you don't usually think about? Were any of your thoughts negative? When you have a negative thought, you can use mindful skills to reduce the power that thought can have. Use any of the following mindful skills to help:

- **Do the dropping-in practice.** Be aware of your body, breath, and mind. Notice your body, your breath, and your mind—both the thoughts and feelings that are arising. Become more aware of what negative thoughts are coming up.

- **Don't believe everything you think.** Just because you think something, it doesn't mean it is true, real, or factual. You can notice the thought; tell yourself, "Oh, interesting; that's what I'm thinking right now"; and then move on to another topic.

● **Be Velcro to the positive and Teflon to the negative.**
   You don't have to let the negative self-talk stick. You
   can use STOP to help.

All of these skills use the power of directed mindful
awareness to learn about the content of your thoughts,
to help you to be in the now, and to move forward without getting stuck in the negative.

MINDFUL TAKEAWAY

One of the key practical lessons of modern neu-
roscience is that the power to direct our attention
has within it the power to shape our brain's firing
patterns, as well as the power to shape the archi-
tecture of the brain itself.

—Daniel J. Siegel, psychiatrist

39

MINDFUL PAUSE

Mindfulness puts a space or pause between a stimulus and a response. It is in this space that reactivity and impulsivity decreases and thoughtful responding ensues.

taking space: a mature time-out

Children are often put in time-outs when they are in trouble. Time-outs get a negative rap because many people associate them with this childhood experience, but the idea of taking a time-out when you need it can be very helpful.

There is nothing wrong with choosing to take space, which is a mature time-out. When you feel emotional—angry, frustrated, sad, overwhelmed, and the like—there is no reason you can't take some space to collect yourself. If you are trying to make a decision, taking space also gives you time to figure out what you want to do.

take a mindful pause

When you take a pause before responding to yourself or others, you allow for a response instead of a reaction. A mindful pause can also help reduce reactivity and impulsivity. Here are some examples of ways to take a mindful pause:

- Notice one entire breath (an in-breath and an out-breath).

- Count breaths (breathing in one, breathing out one; breathing in two, breathing out two).

- Pay attention to any of your five senses (sight, sound, smell, touch, and taste) in the moment.

- Take a walk.

- Notice the physical sensations and cues your body is giving off.

decision making: play out the end of the movie

Think of a decision you are trying to make. Take a pause and think, "If this were a movie, how would the movie end?" Use this tool when you have to make decisions. If you play out your decision as if it were a movie, you will most likely be able to imagine what will happen. For example, it is 1 a.m. and you are enjoying chatting with a new romantic interest but realize you have to get up at 7 a.m. You want to keep chatting, but you know if you do you are going to have a really hard time getting up in the morning and functioning during the day.

Let your movie ending guide your decision.

MINDFUL TAKEAWAY

When you are making decisions, consider taking a mindful pause. Doing so can create a space and allow for a thoughtful response rather than an impulsive reaction.

40

MINDFULNESS IS ABOUT NOTICING YOUR FEELINGS

When people say, "I think I feel . . . ," they are expressing a thought, not a feeling. For example, if you ask someone how he's feeling and he responds, "I think I feel sad," that is a thought. Look out for this wording to see if you sometimes fall into the same trap. It is normal, but it does not get at your true emotions.

naming your feelings

Most people don't have an extensive feelings vocabulary. They may describe their feelings in basic terms—for example, *sad*, *mad*, *angry*, *happy*, or *glad*. It can be difficult to identify your feelings if you don't have a word that accurately matches how you feel. The following is a list of twenty-five terms to expand your feelings vocabulary. You may already use some or all of them, but having them here in one place can help when you can't quite put your finger on what feeling you're having.

FEELINGS VOCABULARY				
Thrilled	Grateful	Hopeless	Miserable	Terrified
Excited	Playful	Depressed	Helpless	Furious
Fantastic	Calm	Despairing	Hurt	Resentful
Delighted	Peaceful	Grieving	Worthless	Irritated
Loving	Chill	Distressed	Guilty	Ashamed

why it is important to know how you feel

People are taught to pay more attention to their thoughts than to their feelings and bodies. That doesn't really make sense, since thoughts, as you have learned, can be wrong. How you feel physically and emotionally are much stronger indicators of how you are actually doing from one moment to the next.

The skills presented in this book ask you repeatedly and in different ways to open your awareness to how you are feeling physically and emotionally. Through these mindfulness-based practices you can expand both your spacious and directed awareness to all that exists in the moment—not only to your five senses and thoughts, but also to your physical sensations and emotions.

Sometimes you can't put your finger on exactly how you are feeling because it is a physical sensation—prickly, irritable, edgy, or uncomfortable. You feel something, but you can't seem to find the words to describe it. This is normal. Your body holds a lot of how you feel emotionally. It isn't like your body and feelings get to reside on different planets; they are in you equally at the same time. They just don't often get as much attention as your thoughts do. To assess your overall state of being at any one moment, check in with the following:

- What your thoughts tell you

- What emotions you are feeling

- What physical sensations you feel in your body

Knowing how you feel helps you navigate your life and provides you with much-needed information. Here are some examples:

- It helps you with decision making.

- It enables you to respond to people, places, things, and situations instead of reacting.

- It alerts you to whether you feel safe or threatened.

- It alerts you to whether you feel satisfied or dissatisfied.

- It tells you whether you're feeling connected or not.

- It helps you observe and process information.

- It gives you a sense of power, control, and agency to know your feelings at any given moment.

MINDFUL TAKEAWAY

Knowing how you feel at any one moment, physically or emotionally, provides you with the necessary information to assess your state of being, make decisions, and move through your day-to-day life.

41

MINDFULLY TELL SOMEONE HOW YOU FEEL

When you mindfully tell someone how you feel, you do so after you have thought it out and perhaps taken some space—a minute, a mindful pause—maybe only a second or two. Mindfully telling someone how you feel reduces mistakes by giving you the space to consider the impact of what you are going to say and allows you to respond rather than react.

use MI-Messages to tell someone how you feel

MI-Messages are a way to mindfully express your feelings to another. MI-Messages have two parts:

PART 1: Mindful check-in. Start by mindfully checking in with how you feel physically and emotionally; notice what thoughts are arising. Use any of the mindfulness skills you want to center yourself in the now—for example, notice your five senses, do a quick dropping-in practice, check in with your breathing, or pay attention to your grounding focal points.

PART 2: I-Message. Use the following formula to tell someone how you feel:

When _____ (the behavior)

I feel _____ (the feeling)

Because _____ (the reason)

"When _____ I feel _____

because _____."

example: Matt's message to his parents
"When I can't text after ten at night, I feel frustrated because my friends get to text later."

This doesn't mean that Matt will get to text after ten, but he has let his parents know how he feels.

example: Ana's message to her group of friends
"When you told other people about my getting fired from my job, I felt hurt and frustrated because I didn't want people to know."

In this example, Ana was able to tell her friends how their actions caused her to feel. She didn't attack them. Also, telling them how she felt might mean they won't make the same choice in the future.

the power of using MI-messages

MI-Messages are a way to tell someone how you feel without attacking or judging them. When you use MI-Messages, you are coming from a personal place of how the other person's actions caused you to feel. No one can tell you that you don't feel the way you do. You have the right to feel however you feel at any given moment. Because you are speaking from your own feelings and have given mindful thought to it, your MI-Message is more likely to be heard by the receiver than if you were to react automatically without mindfully thinking it through or knowing your true feelings.

MINDFUL TAKEAWAY

MI-Messages allow you to tell someone how you feel without being verbally aggressive. Because you are coming from a place of how you feel, no one can say that it isn't the way you feel. You have a right to your own feelings.

42

ASSERT YOURSELF

Being respectful to others doesn't mean you have to accept everything they say or do. You can assert yourself by telling them how you feel.

assertive communication

There are four types of communication styles: passive (lacking action), assertive, aggressive (attacking), and passive-aggressive (backhanded) communication. Assertive communication is the only one that is particularly beneficial. It is a way of speaking that conveys respect for yourself and others while also maintaining your needs, wants, and beliefs. This can be very hard to do in practice. People are often afraid to assert themselves for a number of reasons:

- It can be hard to do.

- They may feel bad.

- They might hurt the other person's feelings.

- They may not be in line with what the other person wants them to do or believe.

- It means they have to say, "No," or "No, thank you."

- It doesn't go along with the majority opinion.

positively asserting yourself

You are positively asserting yourself if you state, express, defend, maintain, or put into action your needs, wants, and beliefs by being honest and respectful. People might not agree with you, but by being assertive, you are respecting yourself. You are letting yourself and others know that you have value and that you matter. You are also modeling for others how to assert themselves.

Here are some examples of asserting yourself:

- Recognizing that your needs are just as valuable as the needs of others

- Knowing that it isn't selfish to take care of yourself and practice self-care

- Realizing that there are times when it is important to put yourself first

- Clearly expressing what you want or need from another person

- Clearly expressing what you want or need for yourself

- Knowing your limits and the boundaries you don't want crossed

- Knowing what actions and behaviors you are not willing to tolerate from others

- Not putting yourself in vulnerable or uncomfortable situations

- Saying no or leaving if you are in a vulnerable or uncomfortable situation

- Knowing what you want or need in a given situation

MINDFUL TAKEAWAY

Acknowledge, honor, and state your wants, needs, and beliefs as ways to assert yourself. Don't forget that when you assert yourself, you are also showing self-respect. You are telling yourself that you matter.

43

MINDFUL BUBBLE

When you are having a disagreement with someone, imagine there is a bubble around you. Think of this imaginary bubble as space between you and the other person. It can also give you the opportunity to pause before you respond.

manage conflicts with people: the four Rs

Below is a four-step process for managing difficulties and conflicts with other people:

STEP 1: Recognize. Identify the conflict or difficulty.

STEP 2: Reset. Don't react.

STEP 3: Resource yourself. Assess your resource levels for safety, satisfaction, and connection.

STEP 4: Respond. Take appropriate action, if action is needed.

STEP 1: Recognize. This is a huge first step. Sometimes it can be hard to even realize you are in a conflict and determine whether it is hard on you physically or emotionally. Notice that there is a problem, and go to step 2.

STEP 2: Reset. Before letting your thoughts or emotions take over, or when you notice the automatic impulse to react, hit your reset button. Take a mindful pause or take some space for yourself.

STEP 3: Resource yourself. Chapter 20 included a quotation from Rick Hanson that people's fundamental needs are to be safe, satisfied, and connected. Consider which, if any, of your fundamental needs for safety, satisfaction, or connection are being activated by this conflict and need resourcing. Assess what resources you have and use them to help with this conflict.

Safety

- Are you being threatened verbally or physically?

- Are you in physical or mental pain?

If you are experiencing either, you need to take yourself out of the situation as quickly and safely as possible. If you are feeling weak, helpless, scared, frightened, alert, or fearful, you also need to try to remove yourself from a potentially harmful situation. If you feel the situation is tolerable—for example, if you are having an argument—consider resetting, taking a pause, and continuing the conversation at a later point. It is important to err on the side of caution to keep yourself safe!

Satisfaction

- Are you feeling disappointed?

- Are you feeling wronged?

- Are you feeling like you have lost something?

- Are you feeling regretful?

- Are you unhappy?

These feelings indicate that you aren't satisfied with someone or are wishing the situation with them could be different. It is important to consider telling this person how you feel, asserting yourself and using MI-Messages. You have a right to feel satisfied in your relationships.

Connection

- Are you feeling left out or excluded?

- Are you feeling let down?

- Are you feeling lonely?

- Are you feeling jealous, resentful, or angry?

These feelings indicate that the connection you have with someone is fractured in some way. Perhaps you are not as close with the person as you would like, or the person is not as close to you as you would like. You have the right to feel included, respected, wanted, and appreciated. If you aren't feeling connected, you can assess the importance of the relationship. Take time to savor the relationships in which you do feel connection.

STEP 4: Respond. Instead of reacting, you are taking the time to choose how you want to respond. You have a few choices on how to respond to the conflict. You can (1) do nothing; (2) change your behavior; or (3) ask the other person to change their behavior. Depending on the situation, any of these choices may be a good way to respond.

MINDFUL   TAKEAWAY

When you have a conflict with another person, use the four Rs to manage the conflict mindfully: Recognize the situation; Reset, don't react; assess your Resources; and Respond to the situation.

44

MINDFUL MESSAGING

Have you ever sent a message or posted something you wish you hadn't? It happens!

send mindful messages

There are five mindful steps that can help make it easier to avoid regrets and mistakes in messaging. These steps can also apply to posting pictures, texting, or sending e-mails.

STEP 1: Think before sending. Ask yourself if you have thought out the message you are going to send.

STEP 2. Consider your Intention. An intention is your reason or purpose for doing what you're doing in the moment. Ask yourself why you're sending the message. Is it well intended? Are you angry, anxious, or upset? Check in on your body for cues, and if it is providing red flags that you are emotional, take a pause and consider waiting a bit.

STEP 3: Don't rush. Just because someone sends you a message, you don't have to respond right away. Maybe you don't have to respond at all. You can take your time when sending and responding to messages. You can ask yourself, "Is it something I need to respond to? If so, when?"

STEP 4: Reread. Reread your message before you post it. Ask yourself if it was thought out.

STEP 5: Pause. Take a second or two before you hit Send or Post to make sure you want to.

surf the urge to post: SOBER

It can be hard not to respond to someone who has upset you, share juicy information or news, or keep up with everyone else's posts and acquire more likes on social media. Before messaging or posting, surf the urge of what it feels like to want to do so right now! Take a minute and go through the process of SOBER (**S**top, **O**bserve, **B**reathe, **E**xpand, **R**espond) created by psychologist G. Alan Marlatt:

STOP: Stop where you are. Be present and tune in to what is actually taking place in this moment.

OBSERVE: Observe how you are feeling physically and emotionally.

BREATHE: Take a deep breath. Center your attention on your breathing.

EXPAND: Expand your awareness. Consider what impact the message or post will have—positive, negative, or neutral.

RESPOND: Make a decision and respond accordingly. Decide if you want to message or post.

You can use SOBER in other situations as well:

- Managing urges and cravings

- Coping with difficult triggers

- Handling high-risk situations

- Making decisions

MINDFUL   TAKEAWAY

Before you hit send or post a message, take a mindful pause. Read your message and ask yourself, "Do I really want to say this?" This can prevent a lot of unnecessary drama.

45

GIVE HARMFUL JUDGMENTS LESS BRAIN TIME

All of us have judgments all the time. It is a normal part of being human. A judgment is a type of thought. It involves assigning some value to situations, defining them as good or bad, right or wrong. Once a judgment persists long enough, it becomes a belief.

Think for a minute or two, and write down any judgments as they come to your mind on a piece of paper. Next, think of some of the judgments you have about yourself. Finally, think of some of the judgments you have about other people. Ask yourself, "Are my judgments about myself or others real, true, and factual? Is there any evidence to support them? Or are these judgments untrue or fake?"

helpful judgments

Many judgments you have during the day are actually helpful:

- **They allow you to process information more quickly by relying on your memory of how to complete a task.**
  example: You make soup from a can quickly because you have done it before. You know what items you need and how to do it.

- **They allow you to make decisions quickly based on experience.**
  example: You can choose a can of soup you like based on your memory of how it tasted before.

- **They alert you to harm or danger.**
  example: You know if you touch the burner, you will burn yourself. If you accidentally touch the pot handle and it feels hot, you know that part of the pot isn't heat resistant, and you don't continue to touch it.

harmful judgments

Judgments are harmful when they make you feel negative about yourself, others, places, things, or situations. Harmful judgments are not necessarily true, real, or factual. Just because you make a judgment, you don't have to believe it. The characteristics of harmful judgments are as follows:

- **They are not true, real, or factual.**
  example: Believing the world is flat although there is proof it's round.

- **They are based solely on your own beliefs or values or those of others.**
  example: Deciding that people have no taste in music if they don't like the bands you do.

- **They are about performance, appearance, behaviors, actions, ability, age, speech, and worth.**
  example: Disliking all people who have dyed their hair blue because your friends don't like people with blue hair.

mindful judgment journal

You can let go of a lot of added stress, pain, and suffering by learning to notice and free yourself from your harmful judgments. Harmful judgments are usually automatic and may feel natural to you. To make changes in this area, you can work on being mindfully aware of your judgments, and when you notice a harmful one, you can make a note about it in a journal. Follow the four steps of the mindful judgment journal exercise below.

STEP 1: Notice a harmful judgment.

STEP 2: State and/or write down the harmful judgment. If you know what makes it harmful, state or write that.

STEP 3: Be open, gentle, kind, and curious about the judgment ("Oh, interesting; this is the judgment I am having right now").

STEP 4: Check in with your breathing and how you feel in your body.

After going through this process, do you have any key insights about being mindful of your harmful judgment? Reflect on how you feel now.

MINDFUL TAKEAWAY

Awareness that a judgment is harmful can lead to change. If you can increase how often you notice a harmful judgment, you can decrease its impact and the number of harmful judgments you have about yourself or others.

46

SOMETIMES A PAIN JUST WANTS TO BE HEARD

Jon Kabat-Zinn wrote, "If one hopes to grow in strength and wisdom and bring healing into your life, you must realize that every moment is precious even if in pain."

Sometimes people are in physical or emotional pain and don't even notice it. Scan your body from the tips of your toes to the top of your head. Do you feel any physical pain that you didn't notice before? Now check in with your mind. What feelings are present right now? Do you feel any emotions that you didn't notice before?

being mindful of your pain
A tumbleweed is a plant that breaks away from its roots and is carried by the wind. As such plants are blown around, they connect with one another to form a larger

tumbleweed. Consider a pot of water that has been placed on a hot burner. If it isn't attended to, the water will eventually boil over.

Pain is like a tumbleweed or a pot of boiling water. It starts off as one thing, one size, and if it isn't noticed, it often gets bigger or even much worse than when it started. Pain is there to alert you and provide you with information. The information might not be pleasant or wanted, but it is information nonetheless.

Being mindful of your pain is to be aware of it and to learn more about it. Once you know about your pain, you can choose what actions, if any, to take; assess what resources you may need; and decide how you want to deal with it. You can use the acronym PAIN (**P**resent, **A**ware, **I**nvestigate, **N**ourish) to help:

PRESENT: Be present to what is causing you pain. Pay attention to the pain. Notice that it exists.

AWARE: Hold the pain in your awareness. Open your thoughts, feelings, and physical sensations to it.

INVESTIGATE: Investigate what resources you have to manage the pain.

NOURISH: Nourish yourself. Fill yourself up with self-care and self-compassion. Notice the parts of you that aren't in pain as well as those that are. Notice what basic needs you have that are being met right now to help shift your perspective. Send heartfulness—warm wishes, kind regards, and thoughts—to yourself, even the parts that are in pain.

pain in your life is inevitable; stress is optional

Physical and emotional pain is inevitably going to occur. It is what you do with the pain, how you manage it, that will inform how stressed you are by it. Stress is optional— the pain doesn't have to be extremely stressful or even stressful at all. The factor that decides how much stress you feel is how you choose to perceive, appraise, and manage the pain. Some people manage pain by blocking it, but blocking behaviors prolong pain. *Blocking behaviors* are negative coping behaviors that people engage in as an attempt to deal with difficult situations. However, engaging in these blocking behaviors often create more pain and suffering. They do not fix problems; they might even make the problem worse. Look at the following list of ways people block pain and a real-life situation as an example.

Lindsey gets dumped by her significant other. Obviously, this is going to be emotionally painful. How Lindsey manages the painful situation and what blocking behaviors she engages in are going to affect her overall level of stress. Below is a list of some blocking behaviors:

BLOCKING BEHAVIORS

- **Push away the pain.**

  example: Lindsey goes out with friends every night. She stays so busy that she almost doesn't have time to think about the breakup happening.

- **Deny what happened or pretend it doesn't exist.**

  example: She doesn't tell people that she and her partner have broken up. Even though it is upsetting, she doesn't want to accept it.

- **Hold on to or cling to the pain.**

  example: When Lindsey starts crying, she puts their favorite music on repeat. It makes her feel worse.

- **Ruminate on or obsess about the pain.**

  example: She can't stop thinking about how she isn't good enough and what she did wrong to make this happen. She keeps going back over her messages from the last few months of their relationship.

- **Engage in negative self-talk and focus on harmful judgments (I should have done this. I could have said that. I would have done this. Why didn't I do this?").**

  example: Lindsey wants to know what she did wrong. She starts saying, "I'm ugly. I'm fat. I'm a loser If only I looked like Jenny, I wouldn't have gotten dumped."

- **Feel guilt or shame about the pain.**

  example: She thinks the breakup is all her fault and feels bad about it.

You can probably see that nothing positive comes out of any of these blocking behaviors. Lindsey isn't managing her pain at all, and blocking the pain is hurting her even more—causing her more stress.

MINDFUL   TAKEAWAY

The more you attach to, pull toward, push away from, or avoid the pain, the more pain and suffering you experience. Being mindful of pain can prevent unnecessary pain, stress, and suffering. Use the acronym PAIN (Present, Aware, Investigate, and Nourish) to help you mindfully manage the pain in your life.

47

IT IS SO SILENT IN HERE

Turn your electronic gadgets off, or at the very least, put them on silent. Sit for one minute with as few distractions as possible. After doing so, ask yourself the following questions:

- Was it actually silent?

- Were there ambient noises?

- Was it difficult to be and sit in silence?

- Was it uncomfortable to be and sit in silence?

- What thoughts were present?

- Were my thoughts about anything different from my usual thoughts?

● What feelings came up when I was asked to turn off
   or silence my electronics?

types of silence

How often you are in absolute silence? The truth is almost never. There are two types of silence: real silence
and perceived silence.

Real silence is the space from one noise you can hear
to the next. This space may last only a second or even
a millisecond. *Perceived silence* is when it seems silent
to you, but it isn't. People often think it is silent because
there are no usual noises, like those from people, tele-
visions, computers, music, or phones. However, even
when all those things are taken out of the equation,
there is still noise. Silenced phones vibrate, and computers hum. There are also noises that come from typically
unnoticed things—a whooshing air vent, the fridge mo-
tor running, plumbing noises, sprinklers, an airplane fly-
ing overhead, birds chirping, leaves rustling, and so on.

You can be mindful and do mindfulness practices
during real and perceived silemce. You can acknowledge the sounds that are present—even if it's just air
blowing through a vent—and return to the mindful
practice.

How to Be Mindful of Silence

Mindful silence is the ability to be in the moment, aware
of what you hear, and to notice what you hear and decide where you want to direct your attention. You can

tune in to the sounds around you, or you can notice the sounds and acknowledge them but choose to direct your attention elsewhere—perhaps on what you were doing before you heard the noise.

Mindful silence involves three parts:

PART 1: Being aware of what noises are present

PART 2: Accepting what noises are present

PART 3: Attending or not attending to the noises that are present

silence can feel uncomfortable

It isn't necessarily comfortable or easy to be alone with yourself, your thoughts, or your feelings. Building a muscle of aloneness and turning inward can help provide space for new things to be revealed. Silence can help you tune in to thoughts and feelings—physical and emotional—that can go unheard because of the constant interruption of input and noise from people, media devices, and the like.

Silence can be difficult and is often unwelcome; sometimes people don't want to know what they are thinking or feeling. But these thoughts and feelings will come out sooner or later. In a painful situation, it may be better to notice the pain now rather than prolonging it until it gets more painful. It is like a Band-Aid. Do you pull it off slowly or fast? Either way, it is coming off.

silence from electronic devices

"Silence is golden," a commonly quoted proverb, acknowledges the importance of silence. There can be value to having time without noises that distract you, especially those that come from electronic devices. It isn't that these devices need to be off all the time, but having some space without technology can give you a break to think, process, and recharge without the constant interruptions of vibrations, dings, and pings. A sound break can give you the needed space to make decisions and to decide how you want to respond to a given situation.

MINDFUL TAKEAWAY

Mindful silence can give you the needed space to make decisions about how you want to respond to a given situation.

48

DON'T SWEAT IT

The psychotherapist and motivational speaker Richard Carlson wrote, "Don't sweat the small stuff . . . and it's all small stuff." Think about what is bugging you right now. Ask yourself, is it worth sweating or stressing about? Can you let go of any of it?

awareness of your stuff

Your "stuff" are the stressors that are causing you pain, stress, and suffering. Awareness of your stuff—that which is stressing you out—can be hard enough, and accepting and letting it go can feel like an impossible feat—but it can be done. Many people opt not to be aware of the stuff in their lives because it is sometimes easier *not* to be aware of something in the moment. The poet Thomas Gray coined the adage, "Ignorance is bliss." It can be hard to pay attention to what is difficult or painful. It takes a lot of courage and strength to be aware of your stuff.

By becoming more aware, you can begin to work on accepting and letting go of those things that are weighing on you. Writing down what is occurring in your life can be very helpful when you are working on letting go of the stuff, big or small, that is causing you pain, stress, or suffering. Right now, take an inventory of the different areas of your life—the people, places, things, and situations causing you difficulty. List or write notes about what is occurring in each area. Reflect on the people in your life, the issues you have, the activities going on, and your responsibilities. Pay specific attention to any that are particularly stressful or painful for you.

acceptance

Once you know what your stuff is, can you accept it? Accepting means giving admittance to or approval of what is going on in your life right now. The opposite is ignoring or denying something that is, in fact, real and happening currently. A quotation from the psychotherapist Russ Harris sheds some light on what acceptance means: "Acceptance does not mean putting up with or resigning yourself to anything. Acceptance is about embracing life, not merely tolerating it. . . . It means fully opening yourself to your present reality—acknowledging how it is, right here and now, and letting go of the struggle with life as it is in this moment."

letting go

Past and current hurts and injustices have a way of sticking around, weighing you down physically and emotionally, and they can prevent you from living your life fully. Letting go of something doesn't mean that thing didn't happen, and it doesn't imply that you forgive the person or event. Letting go means allowing for some mental shift, a change in your perspective, about a situation and attempting to change what you are holding on to in some way so it doesn't continue to harm you and prevent you from being happy. Take one problem on your list that has been bugging you and work on letting it go by following these five steps:

STEP 1: Awareness. Be aware of the problem that is causing you some sort of pain, stress, and/or suffering.

STEP 2: Acceptance. Accept and acknowledge the reality of the person, place, thing, or situation right here, right now. What is the truth about it? What is the reality of it? What are the facts about it?

STEP 3: Rightsizing. Work on not blocking or adding more emotion and energy to the problem. What might be making it bigger or smaller than it has to be? Are there positive things you could be doing differently that would help you make the problem more manageable and tolerable?

STEP 4: Relinquishing control. You can't control other people. If you have been trying to manage a problem you don't have control of, remember to use STOP.

STEP 5: Letting go. Have awareness of the problem that is causing you pain, stress, or suffering, accept what it is, make sure you are not making more of it than you have to to right-size it, let go of controlling the uncontrollable, and look at it with fresh eyes. These five steps can help you begin to let go.

MINDFUL TAKEAWAY

Letting go is a process of moving forward and shifting your perspective about a person, place, thing, or situation. Letting go doesn't mean you forget something or forgive someone. It means you free yourself from unnecessary pain, stress, and suffering that is weighing you down.

49

CARING VERSUS WORRYING

A worry can take up so much mental space and time in your life. The author Mark Twain expressed it this way: "I've lived through some terrible things in my life, some of which actually happened."

Here's a life lesson for you: *worrying will not change how something went or how something will turn out.* It won't get your to-do list done or change someone else's or your problems. Worrying is a drain on your time that doesn't provide any kind of helpful result. It can be hard to realize that worrying doesn't accomplish anything, but this realization can allow you the space to put your time, energy, and effort into doing things that can change the result

the worry bully
Worries are like bullies. A bully wants to take some of your time and energy, to get a rise and reaction out of

you. A bully who doesn't get something from you generally moves on. The same is true of worries. A worry wants to bug you, to take up your time, but you don't have to give it space or energy just because it presents itself. You can simply notice it and say, "Oh, this is the worry I'm having right now."

People mostly worry about the past—things that have already happened and can't be undone—or the future—how things will turn out. When you are worrying, you aren't being mindful and in the now. If your attention is being brought into a focus on the past or the future, you aren't getting the opportunity to experience the current moment, the "now."

caring and planning instead of worrying

As much as you might want to change how things will turn out for you, your friends, or your family, worrying will not do this. Caring about an outcome is not the same as worrying about it. Caring is a feeling about someone or about how you would like something to work out. When you worry, you are just ruminating in your own head—and then the worry bully wins.

It is great to care about the people in your life, but there is a line between caring and worrying. You can listen to your friends, give them a shoulder to cry on, and be there for them, but don't let others' problems consume your life. And when you have a problem of your own, don't keep it all inside. Let those in your support system be there to care for you.

What are you worried about in your life right now? Take some time to think of the people and things you are worried about, and write them down. Ask yourself if worrying about these things is changing the situation. Decide which worries you care about and plan steps you can take to make a change. Planning is not the same as sitting there worrying. It is taking action. It puts you in the driver's seat of your life.

MINDFUL TAKEAWAY

Worrying doesn't provide you with any result. Instead of worrying about your past or future, live in the now by doing something that provides a result, like making plans to change what it is you are worried about.

50

MAKING A FRESH START

Every day you have the opportunity for a fresh start. You don't need to let anything from yesterday affect you negatively today. Think to yourself, "Is there anything from yesterday clouding my day today? If so, can I let it go?" Yesterday is over. Be in the present with a new day today.

don't get stuck in your stories

If you were hurt by someone or don't like how you acted in a certain situation, you can often get stuck living in the past. You create a memory of what happened, like a story. Narrative stories are the contents of your past; some are true, but more often they are based on judgments about yourself, someone else, or a situation.

These narrative stories can hold you back from living in the now. When your belief about the past affects how you form current relationships, how you put trust in others, or when it hinders your belief in yourself and your abilities, you lose your freedom to be in the moment. Mindfulness helps you step away from your past and get you out of the stories you tell yourself that hold you back. It brings you into the moment.

Can you think of what is holding you back from accomplishing your wants, dreams, and goals? Are there people who have hurt you? Are there situations that didn't turn out the way you wanted? Are there situations you deny or feel ashamed or guilty about? The answers to these questions can often shed light on what is holding you back. Because something happened once doesn't mean it will happen again or that change isn't possible. *Every day* you have the opportunity to write a new story, make your own way, and forge your own path!

be on your own side

If you do the lessons and practices in this book, continue to use them over and over again, and turn to the parts that really stand out to you at appropriate moments, then you will have the skills to allow yourself to live life on your own terms and take good care of yourself. There is nothing wrong with caring about yourself, loving yourself, and taking care of yourself. Here is a list of ways to be on your own side:

- Acknowledge your strengths and abilities.

- Celebrate your successes.

- Know that there is more right with you than there is wrong at any given moment.

- Plant seeds (practice self-care) and pull weeds (eliminate things or people that are harming you or bringing you down).

- Do things that nourish and fill you up rather than drain or deplete you.

- Talk to yourself like you would to a best friend.

- Reflect on those people who care about you.

- Have self-compassion.

- Notice the things you are grateful for right now, even if they seem really minor.

- Pay attention to your grounding focal points (fingers, hands, feet, breath, and heartbeat).

- Pay attention to your five senses and savor whatever is sweet.

- Increase positive self-talk and decrease your negative inner critic.

MINDFUL TAKEAWAY

To be mindful is to be present to what is—
sometimes pleasant, sometimes unpleasant—and
to walk through life with open eyes, ears, and
heart. If you walk through life this way, you can
experience it in the present moment mindfully.

ACKNOWLEDGMENTS

I started on a journey of inquiry fifteen years ago with this question: if mindfulness works so well for adults, why not bring it to youth—specifically teenagers? I can now look back at what was the start of a full-fledged movement in bringing mindfulness-based work to youth in educational, clinical, and community settings.

I began my work in this field young, green, ambitious, and full of perseverance and determination. Mindfulness would be impactful and meaningful. I knew it in my gut. A few of us embarked on this journey not knowing where it would take us. I would like to honor those who also started in this way alongside me: Laurie Grossman, Amy Saltzman, Susan Kaiser Greenland, Randye Semple, Wynne Kinder, Richard Brady, Irene McHenry, Rob Wall, Diana Winston, Lidia Zylowska, Angela West, Jasmin Zeger, Theo Koffler, Deborah Hammond-Ingalls, Paul Jones, Matt Biel, Jennifer Cohen Harper, and Cator Shachoy. I take a deep bow to you for the work you have done and continue to do today.

To my first teachers and those who were at the start of my journey of mindfulness and the Mindfulness-Based

Stress Reduction Program: Shauna Shapiro, Amy Saltzman, Mark Neenan, Jon Kabat-Zinn, Saki Santorelli, Kirk Warren Brown, Bob Stahl, Florence Meleo-Meyer, John D. Teasdale, Zindel V. Segal, and Mark G. Williams.

To two of my teachers, friends, and mentors who have had the largest imprint on my writing this book. They have a profound impact on my current purpose and intentions for this work, on writing, and on the future trajectory for my work in mindfulness-based practices and positive neuroplasticity: Thank you, Rick Hanson and Dan Siegel.

I have been deeply affected by the teens who have had the courage to open up and have had the willingness to share their lives with me—their pains, struggles, joys, and successes. To all the teens I worked with at the Santa Teresa facility of Kaiser Permanente's Department of Child and Adolescent Psychiatry. Also, a heartfelt thanks to the teens I have most recently had the opportunity to work with and learn from through Mindfulness Everyday and iBme at the 2016 Toronto Teen Retreat and those teens who attended the short teen retreats at the Center for Developing Minds.

To those who made this book possible: Eden Steinberg, Jon Kabat-Zinn, Beth Frankl, Breanna Locke, Karen Schader, Jonathan Green, and Oliver Glosband.

To my current tribe: Steve Brashear, Donna DiGiorgio, Lee Freedman, Ana Floriani-O'Sullivan, Kerri Mahoney, Monica McBride, Laurie Grossman, Susan Brashear-Yax, Stacie Cooper, Alan Kuhn, Mary Rothwein, Todd

Corbin, Dave Sullivan, and Rob Pollochack. I feel blessed and grateful every day to have these wonderful beings in my life.

I also want to send a big shout-out to the teen posse at San Luis Obispo High School's Reach club!

APPENDIX

PRACTICE ADAPTATIONS FOR PEOPLE WITH DISABILITIES

A *disability* is a difficulty that restricts one's movements, senses, or activities. There are three widely accepted types of disability: mental health, learning, and physical. Some disabilities are immediately obvious (for example, if someone is in a wheelchair or has a guide dog); others can be unseen (such as difficulty processing information or being overstimulated by one's senses). Every type of disability matters, and although yours may not be mentioned in this appendix, remember that what is most important is to find the mindfulness practices that work for you and adapt them as needed.

Disabilities, Diversity, and Adversity: Finding Your Ability

In addition to the clear disabilities already mentioned, it is important to consider factors that may be present for you. As you navigate your life, you may experience diversity and adversity issues related to gender identity, sexuality, race, class, and ethnicity, to name a few.

There may be times when you go against the majority or hold views different from the mainstream. At least once in your life, if not more, you will be confronted with hardship, pain, stress, and suffering. This book can be like a treasure chest for those moments. There will be at least one, if not many, mindfulness practices to help you even during difficult circumstances.

There Is More Right with You than There Is Wrong

Did you wake up in a bed today, with a roof over your head, clothes on your body, and fresh water to drink? Right now and at any point in your life, even if you are in pain, facing adverse life circumstances, or dealing with a disability, there is more right with you than there is wrong, and reflecting on the basic needs you have right now that are being met can help.

It isn't that a disability won't make your life more challenging at times, but you can learn how to work through that disability rather than struggle against it. Mindfulness practice isn't about focusing on what you aren't able to do. It is about having an awareness of what is already here, and that includes both the capacities you do have and those you don't. Empower yourself to find mindfulness practices that work for you. Tailor these practices to fit your feelings, mood, and interests from day to day.

Mindful Practice

Mindfulness is about having awareness, accepting, and working with what is. You wouldn't want to pound a square peg into a round hole. Similarly, with the practices in this book, do those that work for you and feel right. Sometimes one practice like mindful walking will be a good fit; another time, a practice such as heartfulness might feel better. Picking a practice will depend on many factors that vary daily—the time of day, how much time you have, or how you are feeling. Taking a disability into account when picking a practice is a factor to consider, but not the only one. Stephen Hawking, the theoretical physicist, cosmologist, and author, said, "However difficult life may seem, there is always something you can do and succeed at."

Finding a Mindfulness Practice Match

The following list provides some issues and suggestions for specific practices to focus on or adapt if you are actively working with a disability.

Issue	Suggestions
Wheelchair	Instead of the walking practice, do mindful rolling. Focus on the movements you can do.
Hard of hearing	Start by reading or having someone sign an entire practice to you in advance, then proceed with the practice. Focus on the other senses you have that are heightened for you.
Blind	If you have a guide dog, let your dog be your eyes during a movement practice. Focus on the senses that are heightened for you.

Issue	Suggestions
Depression or sadness	Do more active practices, such as mindful walking and movement. Do fewer internal practices, such as being with silence or focusing on your breathing. If you are feeling depressed, focus your attention on these specific activities or practices: • HALT • Do things that nourish you • Plant seeds and pull weeds • Use MI-Messages • HOT • Hobby: Use INFO • Be mindful of music (not depressing music) • Practice self-compassion • Get out of stuck stories • Pay attention to grounding focal points, specifically your fingers, hands, and/or feet • Practice heartfulness • Practice levels I–IV self-care • Use STOP • Use SOBER • Decrease blocking behaviors • Name your feelings • Get your wants and needs met • Be kind to yourself • Assert yourself

Issue	Suggestions
Sensory (including feeling over-stimulated by one or more of the five senses)	Focus on the sense(s) that feel comfortable to you. After practicing for some time, consider paying attention to the sense(s) that are difficult for you. Focus on your grounding focal points.
Information processing	If you are able, have someone help guide you through practices or explain what is difficult.
Anxiety, panic, and/ or worries; inner critic	Do more active practices, such as mindful walking and movement. Do fewer internal practices, such as being with silence or focusing on your breathing. If you are feeling anxious, pan-icked, worried, or filled with negative self-talk, focus your attention on these activities or practices: • Give harmful judgments less brain time • HOT • Conquer the worry bully • Practice mindful downtime • Count breaths • Play out the end of the movie • Practice self-care activities • Practice heartfulness

Issue	Suggestions
Autistic spectrum disorders	These practices or activities can help you focus on social skills: • Identify kinds of life moments • Use MI-Messages • Be mindful of routine activities • Recognize and name your senses • Pay attention to grounding focal points
Attention deficit hyperactivity disorder (ADHD) and general problems with attention, focus, and distractability	While having difficulties with attention and focus, try guided practices and keep your practice time short. Try these activities or practices: • Practice mindful walking and mindful walking with photography • Try the dropping-in mindfulness practice • Take a mindful pause • Pay attention to your grounding focal points and practices that are grounding to you • Pay attention to your fives senses • Use STOP • Use SOBER

Issue	Suggestions
Addiction to social media	Here are some practices specific to people who are online a lot: • Notice urges to surf social media • Surfing the urge • Look up from the device • Mindful messaging • Call someone instead of messaging • Practice mindful downtime • Take a mindful pause • Put yourself in a mindful bubble
Anger, frustration	If you are feeling angry, try these activities or practices: • Take a mindful pause • Use the four Rs • Drop in and anchor your stress waves • Pay attention to your grounding focal points • Use STOP • Use SOBER • Use HALT • Practice mindful walking and movement • Put yourself in a mindful bubble • Play out the end of the movie • Use MI-Messages • Practice heartfulness • Practice self-compassion

Issue	Suggestions
Trauma	If trauma is part of your story, do not focus your practice time on silence or breathing. Try these activities or practices: • Pay attention to grounding focal points • Pay attention to your five senses • Practice mindful walking and movement • Practice self-compassion • Identify past-now-future thoughts • Practice self-care • Take a mindful pause
Engaging in self-harm	Here are some practices specifically helpful to people who self-harm: • STOP • SOBER • HALT • Ride the wave • Recognize impermanence • Take a mindful pause • Avoid blocking behaviors • Play out the end of the movie • Practice mindful walking • Grab an ice cube • Put yourself in a mindful bubble

These examples are merely suggestions of activities and practices that may help. If one or more work, continue to use them; if they don't, try others.